Words about the Book...

I find here an openness and sharing that is intensely touching and triggers so many correlations to my own life. I sense a lovely rhythm and balance throughout; the style is consistent, and each segment is pleasantly sprinkled with nuggets of the author's life and experiences from a surprisingly personal perspective. God, I feel I know him and more than that–I like the man that wrote these words. He's interesting and humble and cares a lot about a great many things, and tells these stories with all his heart. Bravo.

–Kay from Kentucky

The short chapters/observations retrain our eye. We see nature, we see ourselves in it. Each chapter removes a bit more of the grime of the machine world to reveal more of the world that I was able to see so clearly as a child. A world full of wonder. A place that I participated in. For by seeing the true world again, we not only "see" it but we can start to inhabit it again. We can return home. This is not a "How to Do" book but a "How to See and Be" book.

–Rob from Prince Edward Island

This moving collection of essays touched me deeply with Fred First's well-written themes that re-connect us all with the treasures of our natural world. He strongly emphasizes the fact that there is no greater gift we can give our children as well.

–Gretchen from Virginia

Author's Note

You will find a few moments of pleasant reading in this book, I trust. More than this, it is my hope that as you look out at my world through my eyes, you will come to know the "Ah, Aha, and Haha" realities in your own life. Looking through this lens at the terrain of your daily life may offer clarity and depth to your seeing, to your understanding and to your caring for the places and people in your own local habitat.

It's a risky business exposing one's thoughts and fears, memories and hopes to strangers. But I'm convinced that from this kind of unselfconscious hyper-local personal story-telling, you'll discover that you and I are not all that different.

In the end, there's no them and us; there's only us. We can and must grow together in our families and communities, building our future upon each other's humor and courage, wisdom and strength of character—now more than ever.

What We Hold In Our Hands

What We Hold In Our Hands
a slow road reader

Fred First

GOOSE CREEK PRESS ~ FLOYD, VIRGINIA

Published by Goose Creek Press
Floyd, Virginia

Digital Printing by Lightning Source, Inc. Copyright 2010

Library of Congress Control Number: 2009923996

Cover and interior Images
by the author

For information, email gckpress@gmail.com or visit
goosecreekpress.com or fragmentsfromfloyd.com

ISBN: 9780977939534
SAN: 8 5 0 – 6 7 4 4

Acknowledgements

For the opportunity to lay out my rambles where folks could read them, I am most appreciative: to the Floyd Press for imposing some regularity to the writing by the biweekly deadlines; to the local NPR station for helping me hone my speaker's voice and cadence.

Thanks to my online readers who were my first audience long ago and without them, if I wrote at all, it would have been merely for the exercise and my own private consumption, no more meaningful or fulfilling than for my photographer's side to take thousands of pictures and leave them in my camera.

I am especially indebted to the graphic design help from Elaine Martinez and editing assistance and friendship of Gretchen St. Lawrence, both of whom have stayed the course through divers technological and temperamental lapses at my end that would have worn down lesser souls.

I am, of course, forever beholding to my wife, Ann, who allowed me the wonderful space to get the job finished once she could see I was going to do again what I'd said I never would, who listened to my roughest drafts and never pretended they were done until they were done.

My great joy is that now I have a new excuse to meet more of you, to hear your stories, and to start a folder for yet another book of days.

Title Page image: slow road barn, pen and ink by Ron Campbell, dreamcatchermeadows.us, Floyd Virginia

Table of Contents

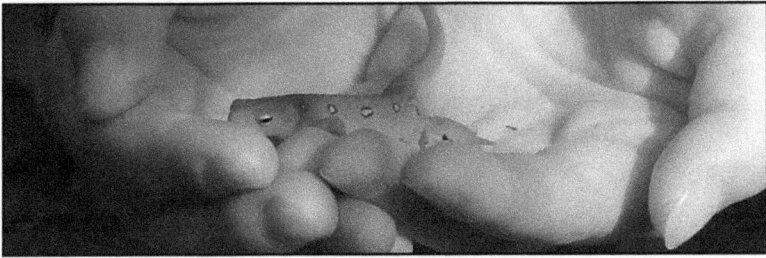

To feel the life pulsing inside the shell of a box turtle's cold hard carapace. To know the tickle of a millipede's "thousand feet" crawling on the back of their hand, or the touch of the red-spotted newt moving on his short legs by wiggling his body in an S-curve left and right against their palm.

What they hold in their hands today—iPod or millipede —can make all the difference in where their center of importance will be in their adult lives.

The fragments of daily life that we may record in words... show, for better or worse, some small truth about our unique place and purpose in this world. Taken together, the trivial threads—a memory, an insight, a hope realized or lost—weave the fabric of our stories. This is what we hold in our hands; we know it well and can speak of it from the heart.

Preface

The 4 a.m. excursion that has brought home ninety-plus personal essays (and other such writings) is an habitual armchair scavenger hunt that starts my day, a bathrobe and slippers field trip powered by curiosity.

It may seem an odd passion to set out every day and so early, even on weekends. But it is my writer's way of sampling the currents of the times, mine and ours.

Sorting these artifacts to find a pattern in the apparent randomness and chaos of everyday living has become a centering exercise that moves me a little closer to an understanding of what it is that you and I together hold in our hands.

These stories and essays range as widely as do daily experience and the winds of my whimsy, worry and wonder. The collection is richly hyper-local, with accounts of living the rural life in the near habitat of home, a small dot on the map that is a microcosm of the Blue Ridge and the southern Appalachian realms.

There are personal stories here, even some from and about our children, and this time around, including more than a few on the action verb, aging, that I have come to know far better in the three years since the first book.

Here too, I share concerns as naturalist for the survival challenges faced by the smallest of our fellow companions who are important harbingers of our planet's health.

We hold in our hands our unique stories past and present, our values and beliefs, our hopes from common culture and experience and out of the same soil, water and air. We hold the fate of our children's world and future.

This book of personal essays is a single grain of sand from a low, green mountain of human experience. It is a peculiar narrative of particular moments and dramas in one life, one family and one pleasantly-rural county and home place.

Throughout this eclectic assortment resonates a joy for living. These pages hold the subliminal hope that all of us will revisit with gratitude the shared blessings in our grasp—our here, our now, our abundant riches of the senses, of memory, of duty and relationship together in a common human family and story.

About the Writing and the Writer

This collection has been growing for a couple of years in my archives, one blog post, one slow-walk AHA moment (you'll hear more about this in Part 9), one news column or radio essay at a time, cell by organ by limb, migrating finally to a comfortable place in the whole of it all.

You'll find some family resemblance between this book and the first book, *Slow Road Home*. Both are compilations of "folk writing" as a blog reader long ago described my style and subject matter. The topic material of both is wide-ranging, even more so in this volume.

This *Slow Road Reader* is a sampler of very different flavors and textures, but the sum of them is also united by a sense of life-long curiosity and humor or sometimes concern, often about very local matters but with wider and more global truths embedded.

You can open this book anywhere, read a passage at random, and have a story without an urgent need to read further to get to the conclusion or resolution. At the same time, you'll find some continuity and theme throughout and between the books. The siblings have the same father, and so share a common ancestry, traits and voice because he has these particular field markings as follows.

Father and grandfather: Find here not a few stories that feature our grand-daughter Abby. There's a Father's Day poem from our son, Nate, and one I wrote to his big sister Holli just before she brought Abby into our lives. And of course there are more than a few that bring in the spousal unit, the hero here of Bonny and Clyde and the Killing Fields of Goose Creek. But I'm still paying for Solomon's Sheets in *Slow Road Home,* so I've tried to be good this time.

Naturalist and teacher: This book, like the first, has nature as its most common theme—a given considering my forty-year history as a biology-watcher and classroom teacher. One way or another, you the reader will be challenged to become an active participant in your particular landscape and to act on the living planet's behalf. There are facts and factoids embedded here and there throughout, and you just might discover some useful truth (or not so useful but interesting just the same) that you didn't know about a common plant or animal in your own back yard.

Believer: ... in the power of humor and personal vision and voice to tell a story best. If you squint your eyes just a little, you'll find me peeking out of every one of these pieces. If you were a fly on the wall watching as I wrote them, you'd see the energy and joy of a story well told (at least as well as I am able to do it) and perhaps become infected with a sense of the thrill of discovery that permeates and powers my morning writing. You may also detect a certain Gary Larsenesque quirkiness to the way I understand the natural world, taking enormous delight in the small beauties and ironies of the ordinary. As an older writer this time around, the topic of aging and the passing of time finds its way here, especially in those passages that deal with the physical demands of rural living.

Citizen/participant: ... of a household, neighborhood, county, region, nation and globe. Almost all of this book is hyper-local in that its parts were written in my slippers for immediate consumption of local readers and listeners. I do make references often to the town or county of Floyd in southwest Virginia and I've not stripped dates from all these pieces, so they are set in time, but the subjects I think will not become soon dated. Taken as a whole, when you finish digesting all ninety-plus morsels herein, you'll have discovered ways that my story is your story. My hopes and concerns belong in some way to many of us for all our short durations here.

Photographer: I know a lot of folks were expecting more pictures in the first book. I'd love to have had color in this one, but couldn't figure out how to do that economically. But I just had to have more pictures this time around since so often, especially on the blog, I write from an image. I trust these small black and whites add something to your experience of the story.

If you're interested in larger-with-color versions, hop over to the Slow Road Reader Gallery at SmugMug by typing http://is.gd/lq9K into your browser.

Finally, regarding organization: Yes, there is some. I placed these disparate pieces into eight categories for the purpose of my own sorting-out. You can find my category "tags" as subtitles below the title of each piece, and read my descriptions of them near the back of the book. See "Knowing Your Endive from your Escargot.

The ten parts of the book each pass through selections from all or most of these topic categories, moving from children in nature, to nature itself, to the local or global environment, to our household economy of not-so-simple country living, and finally back to the personal.

I trust your visit here will increase your grip and expand your grasp of all it is that you hold in your hands. We have much for which to be thankful, and great work ahead of us.

The slower you go, the more you'll see in the outdoors. The more you see, the more you'll wonder. And the more you wonder, the more you will learn and care. Conversely, the faster you go...

1

Bridging the Nature Gap: Leading Them Outdoors
Curious By Nature

Nature was our first classroom, playground, and teacher. Woods and forest, hillside, meadow and shore were fertile soil for young imaginations. Those places offered grown-ups who are now my age a first glimpse of beauty and adventure. Playing in those places left us with a feeling of awe and freedom. We knew wonder as children, but for many, it didn't survive adulthood. We were born with such curiosity in things outdoors. Do you remember?

Maybe your first memory from nature is a caterpillar crawling on the back porch step, or making a wish as you swirled away the thistle-down of a dandelion, spinning until you were dizzy-drunk. You might remember a sunny afternoon chasing butterflies in the park or cupping lightning bugs in your hands on a balmy June evening, or breathing in the smell of a summer thunderstorm and fresh-cut grass.

A woodlot was a wilderness then and we made up the rules as we went along. Hide and seek, tag—you're it! Tie a thread on a June bug's leg. Climb a tree. Find a four leaf clover. Turn rocks in the creek for crayfish, and don't get pinched. Throw pebbles at a can, skip them on the pond, turn them in your hand for flecks of mica or fool's gold.

We find our treasure where our hearts are. One great treasure we possess is earth itself, the landscapes of our lives. We've always known this. But our hearts have moved indoors.

Adult and child alike, we rush through the outdoor world on our way to life inside. There, we are satisfied with nature, infrequently and vicariously browsed by way of dazzling media technologies. These are entertaining but un-nourishing substitutes for the feel of a cool boulder against our backs or the dry-leaf smell of mountain woods in October. While we are curious by nature, less and less is it nature that we are curious about.

We are constantly entertained but not easily awed. For our kids, the ordinary joy of play outdoors no longer competes for their attention or appreciation, and we adults are at least in part to blame. They want to be like us. They do what we do. They become curious about those things that hold our interest, about the things we talk about, the tools we use. They want to go the places we go. We are their guides. They will follow where we lead them.

Parents, grandparents, and anyone who cares for children: let me invite you back out, to rediscover your neglected sense of wonder. To find that still place again. There is this part of you that still lives, waiting. You are the field guide for your children charges. You must go first.

Share what you learn to see again with new appreciation—for their sakes, and for the good it will do you in many ways of heart and soul. You can learn to love being enveloped by and enthralled in nature again.

It is a worthy task—to reconnect body, mind and spirit with the living planet that so needs our respect and care just now. And if you persist in this enjoyable journey, you will be become a capable companion and teacher, able to lead the children in your life back across the nature gap.

Snake Tales: In League Wit De Debil
Earth Companions

"I wouldn't step foot in that pasture again 'til there's snow on the ground if I were you" a concerned Floyd County neighbor told me recently. With the coming of warm weather "snakes hide in that tall grass. You'd better be careful!"

I could tell that fear and loathing of those creatures would make her an unsympathetic listener to my old snake stories. It seemed her feelings about snakes were not altogether different from those of the toothless old gentleman who rolled down his truck window to ask just what was I doing in a wet-weedy ditch along the side of an Auburn, Alabama dirt road long ago.

"I'm hunting for snakes" I said, matter-of-factly. And as he quickly rolled up his window and sped away, he proclaimed "You must be in league wit da debil!"

I assure you, this is not the case, but there was a time even my wife might have thought so.

We were newly married. I had just started my first semester of graduate school, majoring in zoology. The prof of the herpetology class I was enrolled in awarded points for the different snakes, turtles, frogs, lizards and salamanders collected from the neighboring counties. I just happened to be listening to the twelve-noon radio swap shop one day when a caller announced he had a "big ol' snake in a clothes hamper, if anybody wants it." And of course, I did, and brought it home to our college apartment.

This particular gray rat snake was a stout one—five feet long, powerful but mild of temperament as this species typically is. Since it was a weekend, I would have to find room and board for the creature until I could take it in to the prof on Monday and register my easy points. So, I put it in a large Styrofoam ice chest in the closet of our bedroom, and with the lid slightly open and a couple of Ann's huge pharmacy textbooks on top to hold it down securely, we went to dinner in town.

When we returned, my wife of two weeks discovered that, contrary to my assurances to the contrary, the snake had indeed been able to bench press twenty pounds of books. He was now somewhere free-ranging in our apartment. In the next instant, my newlywed bride was doing a little dance of dread in the middle of our bed.

Between gasps she told me "If I'd known! This is what! It would be like! To be married to! A biology major! I'd have married an accountant!" Our future marital bliss required that I find that snake right away, and so I set about the task, reassuring her I'd find it in three minutes. How many hiding places could there be, after all, in a one-bedroom apartment!

I looked high and low. There was no snake in the bathtub, and none behind the couch. There was no sign of it either under the bed upon which my bride bounced in hysterics. Fifteen minutes later and at the end of my rope, I wondered if maybe a flashlight would help. I went to the desk drawer to fetch it, but the drawer wouldn't budge.

Odd it should suddenly be stuck, I thought, and pulled again, harder. The third try, the drawer came open in one synchronized and awful motion as the leading third of a five foot snake shot up and out of the drawer, jack-in-the-box fashion, and stood upright like a cobra mere inches from my face. Confronted so suddenly, so unexpectedly and at such close range, even our brave, young snake-fancier suffered a jolt of sheer white terror (though it took him years to admit this).

Removed from the drawer and securely tied up in a pillow case, our cold-blooded house guest left our apartment that very hour (this being the single stipulation of the marital or-else ultimatum) to reside in a sandy aquarium in the zoology building on campus. By the time I got back home, she had her feet on the floor again, still not fully convinced I hadn't lost other snakes in our bedroom and never bothered to tell her.

Don't be ridiculous, I probably would have told her. But come to think of it, I never did confess to the one that got lose in the Volkswagen. Don't know yet what happened to that one.

Rehabilitating a Fallen Forest Giant
Earth Companions

What's 100 feet tall, disappeared from the forest in your grandparents' times, and may once again cast shade in the days of your great grandchildren?

The answer—American chestnut. Make that 94% American chestnut.
Over three thousand square miles of eastern woodlands from Maine to Florida and from the North Carolina Piedmont west to the Ohio Valley, chestnut was once our dominant woodland tree, a beautiful and economically important constituent of the forest.

Noticed first in 1904, chestnut blight eliminated more than three billion American chestnut trees from the canopy in the following decades. It was the most destructive disease ever to strike American Forests.

Panic logging probably wiped out living trees that some think might have carried resistance to the disease. And the mighty spreading chestnut tree that sheltered Wordsworth's village smithy disappeared from the forest, seemingly forever.

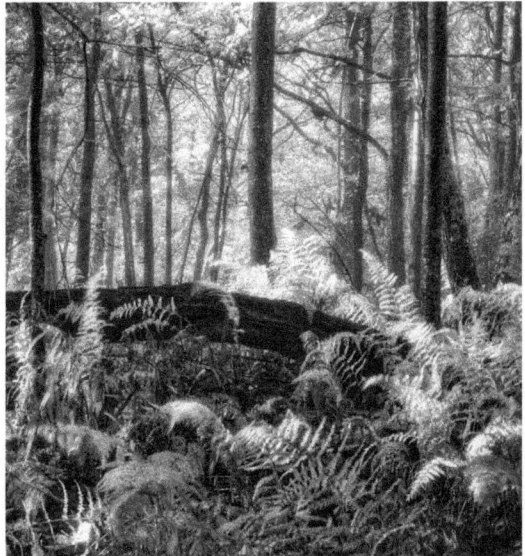

But there is very good news. Persistent genes in stump growth and remnant populations of un-blighted American chestnuts (like the those planted in 1885 in a forest in Wisconsin, beyond the natural range for the tree and the wildfire spread of the blight) carry the tree's "bloodline" into our day.

Hope has returned to the story of this missing majestic member of your grandfather's forest: science has evolved, solutions are at hand.

The genes for blight resistance found in the Chinese chestnut have, with no small effort, patience, expense and skill, been mixed by back crossing with the American genetic instructions found in surviving trees. The resulting hybrid carries 15/16ths (94%) of the original tree's genes.

It is worth noting that much of the work leading up to today's successes in chestnut breeding have taken place nearby—at the research farms of The American Chestnut Foundation in Meadowview, Virginia near Abingdon.

There, only in the past few years, viable trees (in small numbers yet) have been produced that are visibly identical to the American chestnut of 100 years ago but hopefully possessing 100% blight resistance. One such tree was planted on the north lawn of the White House on Arbor Day in 2005 and is reported to be doing very well.

The ultimate hope, of course, is that American chestnut will reclaim its place in the landscape of eastern woodlands: "restoration ecology" the dream is being called. But into that forest dark and deep, miles to go before we sleep.

The availability of chestnuts for future forests is particularly timely as the once-common Eastern hemlocks die (of invasive insect damage) and produce openings in the canopy. As an especially fast growing species, chestnuts rank high for their ability to produce biomass that captures and stores carbon.

But we know very little of the ecological properties of chestnut since forestry science as such did not exist prior to the tree's demise. Native chestnut is fast growing—more so than native black walnut or red oak. What impact its redistribution will have on existing forest species is unknown.

Especially in botanically unique places like the forests of the Smokies, there are laws and regulations that in their present state would prohibit "human interference" or the introduction of a cultivated plant. Will the "new" chestnut be considered a native or an introduced species?

As nursery stock of the new form of American Chestnut becomes available, seedlings will meet high demand. One proposed habitat for planting is on the denuded and theoretically reclaimable flats that were once mountaintops. Experiments in growing chestnut forests on coal mine spoils are already underway.

The return of this native species seems likely, a future reality that will speak to the tenacity of this special tree that against all odds has clung to life for a century, waiting for the care of foresters, scientists and lovers of the natural world who could not bear to live without it in their forests once more.

Local Economies and the Story of Stuff
Within Our Means

Extraction, Production, Distribution, Consumption and Disposal: these are the five ingredients that make up the material-goods portion of our modern US economy—a voracious conveyor belt that carries matter in the things we use from cradle to grave.

The mix of these five steps done the way we do it today is the recipe for consumerism—the American appetite for buying that really became voracious in the fifties. It is the recipe for The Story of Stuff.

Simply stated that recipe reads as follows: (1) Gather the ingredients (mine, log, refine, extract chemicals) (2) Put them together to make something people need or can be made to think they need; (3) distribute portions of it to as many as possible as often as possible; (4) then gobble it up and ask for seconds; and (5) for the considerable amount that's left over, toss it in the trash. Note that #3 and #4 happen here where the stuff is consumed. The other steps, well, they're better done elsewhere because they can be a horribly messy and unpleasant processes.

Not long after WWII, retailing analyst Victor Lebow suggested a plan that would drive the American economy into our times. He said "Our enormously productive economy . . . demands that we make consumption our way of life, that we convert the buying and use of goods into rituals, that we seek our spiritual satisfaction, our ego satisfaction, in consumption . . . we need things consumed, burned up, replaced and discarded at an ever-accelerating rate."

Wouldn't he be proud of us? Consumption on an unprecedented scale is driven by our ravenous appetite, heavily seasoned and appealingly garnished by advertising and made certain by planned or perceived obsolescence and stuff-envy. We always leave the table hungry, no matter how much we eat.

But the planet has become too small a place, and so has our vision of what's involved in our getting and having. In the world ahead, while we can have the things we need, we can't keep getting them by using the old recipe.

We'll need to think with great care about where the ingredients come from, about what portions are enough, and about how the nutrition of our diet of stuff is affecting our health—and the health of other people at the same table called Earth—for the long haul.

The good news: there are lots of points all along this stream of stuff where we can do things better. Perhaps nothing would more improve our reckoning for the side-effects of our over-indulgence than a better understanding of the usually-invisible externalized costs of our hunger for clothes, paper goods, electronics, processed foods and all the other items on our menu.

"If some portion of the cost of producing a product are borne by third parties who in no way participate in or benefit from the transaction, then economists say the costs have been externalized and the price of the product is distorted accordingly. Another way of putting it is that every externalized cost involves privatizing a gain and socializing its associated costs onto the community."— from the *Story of Stuff*

Farm workers (then the local health care system) in California bear the externalized health costs of toxics used to grow that head of lettuce in your refrigerator. The people in a West Virginia creek valley (and the people downstream—we are ALL downstream) bear the costs of taking the top off a mountain for the "clean coal" to produce the "cheap electricity" that powers the light by which you are reading this or the lights left on all night, every night in the high-rise downtown.

Corporate machinery has gotten hung up on efficiency and profits when considering their bottom line. Consumers only see the deceptively low price they pay for a $5 shirt. The costs of cheap are enormous and mostly invisible. We prefer it that way, really.

This kind of re-think could be at the core of what we teach in our schools—in economics, sociology, and civics classes. For an excellent entry point into that discussion, I highly recommend you watch (or download) the *Story of Stuff* written and narrated by Annie Leonard. Better yet, print a copy of the annotated text and share it with folks you talk with at church, work or school in your county.

As we reconsider every aspect of everything we use from start to finish, we will find a recipe that lets us do as well with less, and with the world better off for it. You may pay more for that shirt or those green beans, but in the end, we will all be paying less.

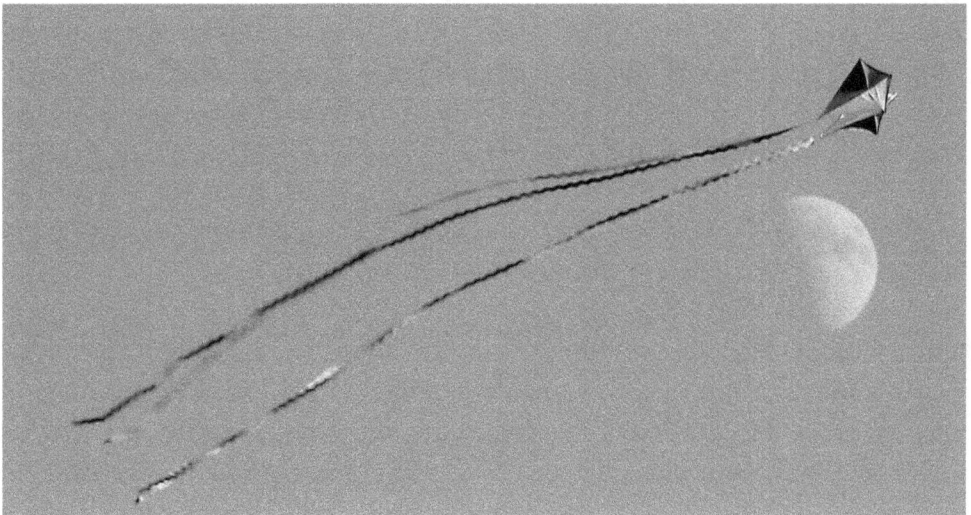

The Foolish Farmer of Erewhon
Neither Fish Nor Fowl

He prepared them lovingly, his favorite mementos and old pressed flowers. He arranged them prominently on benches, near the road. Just beyond, closer to the barn, an oak plank was set across two tree stumps making a crude table to show all manner of clippings and cards that flapped in the breeze—diplomas, certificates and old, yellowed journals.

Someone might care to turn the brittle pages and read the forgotten stories, said the farmer to himself. Up around the bend near the low-water bridge, photographs were pinned haphazardly on the rough trunks of the maple trees—dog-eared, roughly framed or not at all. Some were new, but most were sepia toned from the passage of time, worn with a patina of love and memory.

Trinkets and curios, found things and very private bric-a-brac lined the dirt road along a quarter mile of this seldom-traveled path in a remote part of a sparsely-peopled region of the rural land of Erehwon. Here was more than the eye could take in: cones and seeds; scopes and lensed instruments for seeing things close or far away. There were buckets of garden vegetables and small cages that held insects or small birds or lizards the farmer had tenderly captured, just for a day, so that his visitors could get to know that these things exist in his world—though not in theirs, perhaps. And everywhere wildflowers, mushrooms, liverworts and slime molds—things to the farmer most wondrous and sacred, piled and stacked and scattered.

"Who will come?" she asked derisively. "You are a foolish old man" said the woman, "and if anyone comes, they will think you mad."

"Friends I have never met will come," said the farmer. "Strangers will come who do not know that they wanted to know about these things I show them here until they have seen them. In seeing them, they will see into me and trust me, and we will share the deep things of our souls with each other, me and my visitors."

The farmer was careful to set out chalk boards nailed to roadside trees. He put pads of paper on the display tables so that his guests could tell him about themselves and direct him to their places. With these wonderful leavings, he would be able to visit them all around the world and see their treasures and know their found things, sepia memories, and golden dreams.

And so, the days and weeks passed. Visitors did come down his road, but more often than not, they drove by without stopping. Yet the farmer thought in their passing they might have acknowledged in some small way his racks and tables and adornments. Many came down his road quite by mistake, looking for the shopping mall or in order to read some strange and terrible story not contained in the farmer's collection. Some passers-by surely thought him mad.

But lo, wonder of wonders, some of the wanderers who came tarried, even occasionally handling one or two of the treasures on the rickety tables. They turned them over curiously in their hands. Once a visitor exclaimed "This is the most wonderful thing I have ever seen" upon discovering some small caged creature that was so commonplace in the farmer's life that it was barely worthy of note. This delighted him, and he was eager to tell his wife that indeed, his treasures were becoming treasures to one in a hundred of his guests, and that this was enough. But in truth, he was always disappointed when they remained strangers as they drove away. He soon learned to take joy in the fact that they had come at all.

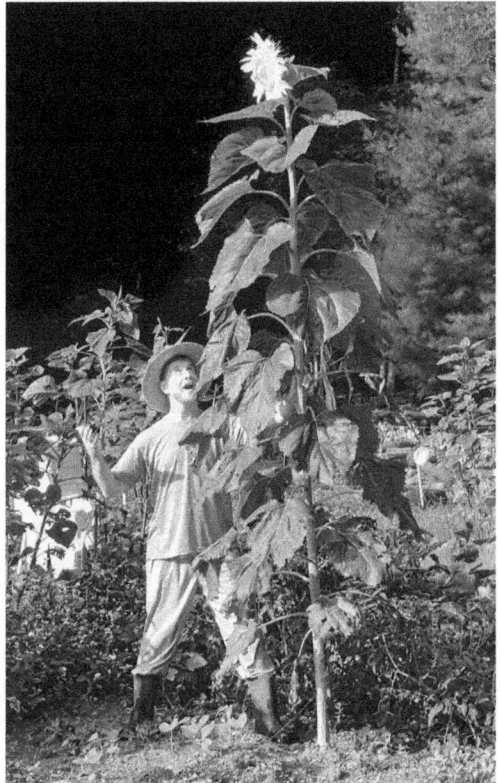

His chalk boards and scratch pads and his green rusty mailbox near the stone walk to his door remained sadly empty. From time to time, a visitor would pen "hello I came by," or "my name is Mary. Nice tables and stuff." The farmer was always thrilled to see that the page was not empty, but dejected when he had given so much of himself and learned so little of his visitors. He began to feel foolish and doubted himself and the public display of his silly yard-sale memories and special things that were sacred only to him.

And yet, in his more hopeful moments, he thought "There is a point to this that I cannot yet see. If I am faithful to my dream, they will come and stop. They will share and invite me to their roads. And when those strangers are able to put their precious things on all the roadsides of Erehwon and the larger world beyond, we will grow to know and trust and care for each other. We will learn from and about those of us that seem strange and unfamiliar, as I must seem now to my visitors."

And so, the strange farmer of Erehwon still searches in his garden and woods, and in his memories and hopes and golden dreams, to find things each day to display before his visitors. If he is mad, he is harmless; and if his strange ways become the way of the lands beyond Erehwon, his madness will have become his joy.

Living Where We Belong
Local Color

My beginnings in place go back to the southernmost tip of the Appalachians in a suburb of Birmingham, Alabama. Even as a child, in their permanence and majesty, the sheltering of mountains brought me a kind of heart-peace.

When we bus-toured the Scottish highlands north of Glasgow, I had a haunting sense that I had lived there before. In a spooky, goosefleshy moment, I pondered the possibility that my mountain roots went back farther in time than I had realized. And sure enough, I discovered this hard fact that connects my Appalachians and the highlands of Scotland and Ireland:

The geologists say that a rock called serpentine begins in the Deep South, underneath those Birmingham mountains that called to me from my grade-school windows. In the far northeast tip of North America at the Gaspe Peninsula, this ancient rock plunges under the North Atlantic and rises again beneath glades and balds of the British Isles. This rocky heart of our ancient mountains gives rise to the same rounded green hills on both sides of the Atlantic.

Is there then a kind of resonance in our souls when we are living where we fit best? For me, that place has always been in the southern mountains. Do you have a kind of land-and-sky in which you feel at home in the deepest sense? Is it mountains or desert, the coast or the heartland prairies?

* Where will your children or grandchildren be called back to when they long for roots and home?

* Did the landscape of your youth leave permanent imprints of place? Will the children in your life have that kind of visceral resonance with the geographies of their lives if they are not immersed in them now while they're young?

* Do we learn to love the one we're with geographically, or do the roots of belonging to place go deeper than caring for what we grow used to?

Those places where our spirit is in harmony with the landscape call to us. Some of us feel at home where we are born; others look for it in places they've never been but long to find. Discovering the source of our sense of place, belonging finally to and in a fixed and particular landscape engenders a kind of relationship. It makes us care for soil and air and water in a deep way we will not feel if the countryside around us is a franchised, faceless and anonymous blur.

Bonny and Clyde and the Killing Fields
Body and Soul Together

The yellow jackets this summer are more abundant and more ill-tempered than I think I've ever known them. Even so, our recent Special Ops maneuver to remove two large nests buried beneath the pasture trail we walk every day seemed just a wee bit over the top—like an absurd, entomological drive-by shooting.

Personally, I'd have just avoided the underground swarms and walked another way around the pasture until winter, but gangsterette Bonnie here wouldn't stand for such cowardice. Here's the way I remember the crime:

As darkness fell, Bonnie and Clyde prepared to make their move, climbing with solemn purpose into the rusted, deer-dented farm-use truck. Tension twisted in their guts—or at least his. There would be dozens of them—hundreds maybe—and it wouldn't do to make a mistake. A slip-up could be deadly. Or at least agonizingly painful. Clyde drove, Bonnie rode shotgun, packin' heat. And she had killin' on her mind.

A few days earlier a farming neighbor at the couple's request became a willing accessory to the crime. In cutting the hay, he dropped a white rag to mark the spot as he tractored past the gang's hideout in a rush, before they could rally an attack en force. The two would come back a few days later for the hit, after the hay had been gathered, after the buzz had settled down and a false peace settled over the colony. The stinging menace by then would have thought the threat had passed.

In the dim light of the evening in question, the pair could barely make out the target. They rounded the bend past the barn and slipped out into the open. Slowly and with grave purpose, the old truck creaked by in the gloom of dusk, weaving between the large round rolls of sweet hay, in space and time closer ever closer to the strike.

The air hung wet, cool, and dead calm; a few bats traced arcs overhead as if it was any ordinary July evening. Just then, Clyde began to sweat with the heat, but more than that with the dread of impending terror and the possibility of suffering—his own, and he wouldn't admit it—the yellow jackets'. He rolled up his window as Bonnie rolled hers down. The time had come.

They pulled along side the target marked by the rag, barely visible in the dim light. Bonnie lifted her weapon, felt its familiar heft, positioned her finger expertly on the trigger for a one-two punch. She was confident; he was not so sure.

The enemy would be quick and fierce in the protection of the turf they had claimed, squatters once hidden in the tall grass. Did they think no one would ever find them there? Now, the grass was gone, they were exposed, edgy. As the truck of doom pulled alongside their neighborhood, they had to know their fate.

Bonnie was a seasoned assassin, determined, steely-eyed, unafraid of pain. Through the open window she fired—a long steady sweeping deadly spray into the enemy's bunker. It seemed to last forever. She was taking no chances. And when the job was done, she doused the place with a half pint of gasoline—a trick learned from her father, disapproved of by her partner. But ties to Family run deep, old habits die hard. To some, the only good bug is a dead bug. Real dead.

"Bonnie" doesn't know it, but there's a yellow jacket's nest in a hole in the bank just outside the garden fence. I've watched with interest as they patrol the squash and beans, and figure they serve a purpose in the overall economy of this place. I'll simply not walk that way until winter comes. And if she does by chance, well, the story of the July massacre is making the rounds; I'll figure they're just getting tooth for tooth.

Your Own Slow Drummer
For the Time, Being

How very different these lovely paramours are as they face to opposite poles in this most intimate of moments.

He, the smaller, has much the bigger eyes proportionally. I wonder if his visual world through green eyes looks different than the same world through her baby blues. Things invisible to her he might see with greatest clarity—a matter of survival, insect aesthetics or sheer male stubbornness.

Ann had sent me on an urgent errand: the dog was running off down the road. I shrugged on my boots in grumbling obedience, and tromped down the front steps, leash in hand.

But wait! "Hey! Check out these fancy flies!" I called back, running inside for my camera.

"The dog's headed down the road, you doof!" she scolded, not appreciating the wonder before me.

"Yeah, but look carefully how different these beauties are. It's called dimorphism," I explained to her. She harrumphed in disgust—a spot-on illustration of marital dimorphism, thank you.

I got no further than this small insect discovery before I was where I was meant to be. But my wife had other plans for me. She frequently loses me on our walks, where for her, getting there is the point. For me, the view each step along the way is more what it's about. We break for spiders; or fancy flies.

Take your time and be willing to drop to your knees and turn over a rock to see what's under it; pluck a twig to scratch and sniff; or simply sit and let your ears listen to sounds smothered by the crunch of your own steps. Look at the ground under your feet. Be a fly on the wall watching yourself watching. Turn up your attention a couple of notches; it's easy to do in the quiet and solitude.

The slower you go, the more you'll see in the outdoors. The more you see, the more you'll wonder. And the more you wonder, the more you will learn and care. Conversely, the faster we go...

Homeland Security: Grandparents on Orange Alert
Within These Walls

"Be safe!" they said. "Stay healthy" friends and co-workers wished us. What blessings more than these could two infrequent flyers hope for? But a touring grandparent is promised neither, and traversing three thousand miles for "in loco parentis" posed unknown risks without guarantees.

That our personal and homeland safety was potentially in jeopardy we heard over the speakers from the moment we entered the terminal. We encountered Orange Security in its bureaucratic embodiment—uniformed, badged and hyper-vigilant—before we could board the plane.

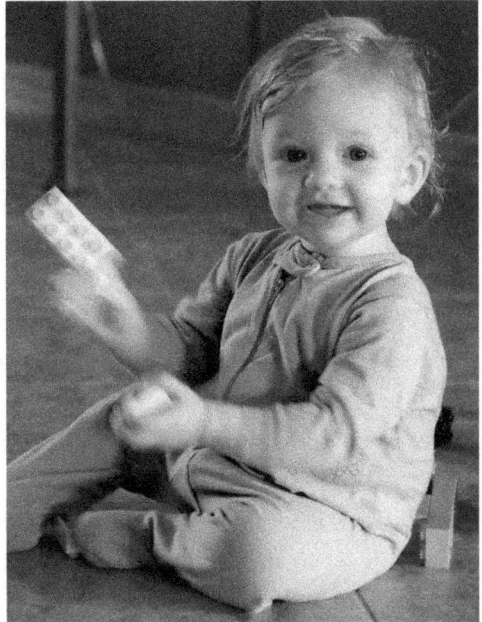

But could there be such a thing as too much safety, I wondered? Surely not when it comes to our children or grand-children. Grandma and I would be in charge of seven year old Abby and nine month old Taryn for four days while their mom and dad celebrated an anniversary with a short trip. Child care: piece of cake. We were seasoned TSA (Toddler Security Agency) pros and what could be so hard about maintaining child health and safety?

Baby gymnastics and perpetual motion, that's what. Our youngest grand-daughter, you see, is not one of those decorator infants that you set in an un-accessorized corner of the rug with a Fisher Price toy and a sippy cup of juice and reposition slightly every fifteen minutes for architectual effect.

In the six weeks since we'd last seen Taryn, she acquired the ability to lunge. She enjoys doing so for the wonderful startle reflex it evokes in the Big People. One totally unanticipated sideways hurtle on the couch, for instance, sent her head-first into her sister's dish of chocolate-syrupy ice cream. A wet wash cloth solved the momentary Code Yellow. We'll look back on this half-gainer some day and laugh.

Second day on duty, it was my watch. Taryn sat with her motors revved at her usual high idle in the high chair at my elbow. I turned my attention for five seconds to her much-neglected older sister Abby who had been on the short end of our attention. Could we go to the water park, please?

I was half-way though my single sentence answer when out of the corner of my eye and in less than a heart palpitation the baby lurched suddenly up and back out of the chair. A this-can't-be-happening filmstrip played for what seemed an eternity as the baby reeled free-falling in slow motion toward the dining room floor. The last frame ended in a sickening thud.

Thanks be for Big Angels (and reassurances from the pediatrician): glossing over the next half hour of red alert and the rest of the day at orange, baby Taryn had sustained not so much as a bump on her head, and who could possibly see our newest gray hairs among so much previously earned?

By day three it was Abby's turn for Dumpa's undivided attention. Let's go out to the swing set in the six foot tall iron-fenced backyard (so sadly sterile by Goose

Creek standards, but outdoors, nevertheless). The cat stalked something invisible in the high weeds just beyond. Abby went over to investigate through the fence.

"It's a snake!" she shouted, screaming at Maggie the cat to get back. The cat used up one of her nine lives, struck at and missed by the fangs of a three foot rattler before we could find a rock to throw—at the stupid cat—a creature for whom a little less curiosity and a little more fear would have meant a lot more security.

Our travel woes went on, but I'll spare you the details. Suffice it to say I was finally feeling that sense of safety and security our friends had wished for us about the time we turned into the driveway back home on the late night of our return—and almost hit a deer.

"The Heart has reasons which Reason cannot know."
— Blaise Pascal

2

Better Without Batteries
Curious By Nature

My best friend Bobby and I were dropped off one Alabama summer afternoon at his Aunt Tink's and told "go play." Though neither of us really knew how to fish, we'd do just that, somehow, in a small creek nearby. We figured it out as we went along and used what we could find close by—a crooked stick, a few feet of sewing thread and a safety pen scrounged from a bedroom dresser drawer. For bait, wild blackberries. Surely fish liked fruit.

We had expected nothing other than small fish to live in a stream like this, so we were both amazed and horrified when a big green crawdad motored out from behind a rock like a tiny robot and carried our hook and berry upstream into the dark shadow of a submerged log. We ran back to the house to tell what we'd just seen.

I remembered this distant fragment of boyhood play while watching our granddaughter Abby create her own excitement and amusement on Goose Creek one afternoon of her summer visit. Her creatures were not as unexpected as the one Bobby and I witnessed, but I feel certain that fifty years down the road, she'll remember her special afternoon of improvised fishing.

A couple of buckets, a few plastic cups and a tiny minnow net: we could not have outfitted her any better for hours of play than with the tools we gathered from around the house for free. We watched from the porch, far enough away that she was in her own private wilderness. We could imagine her thoughts, and some we could hear over the babble of the creek, spoken aloud to the dog.

She was actor, director, narrator and audience as she made up the story about which minnows (and crayfish) and how many of each went in a certain bucket and why. She decided when they had served her secret purpose and could be released—only to be caught from the same sandy pool again several more times before dinner.

Hours pass, she is oblivious. Wet to the knees? She neither notices nor cares. Her plan for the afternoon, to do whatever comes next to mind; and the dog's: to stand ready in the cold water for as long as she might need him.

A place near home. A simple game, she makes the rules. The easy flow of mind and hands. So little space to be for her a wilderness, so vast a time in Abby's eternal present, an afternoon lost in play.

Dragonfly Migration
Earth Companions

The dog and I made one last trip down to the creek at dusk, just to stand and watch the reflection of last light on what water thankfully still flows in Goose Creek. (Actually, the dog was less reflective and chased a Leopard Frog along the weedy banks.)

Wet and energized with his immersion in cold creek water, the pup ran off his invigoration in a stick-tossing romp along his usual play-path between the shed and the rock wall just off the back porch. I think it might have been in throwing the stick up the steep hill that I had occasion to look up. And I was stunned. I lay down on the warm stone pavers to watch the spectacle overhead.

The column of air above the house was thick with them—at least a hundred I could see and many times that beyond the visible limit just before dark.

Coursing, hovering, giving chase, a silent armada of dragonflies zipped and dipped overhead. With their helmet-eyed 360 degree vision, they spun quickly in mid-air, snagging their prey with great precision, a deadly skill and art in their ravenous dance.

With scooping-snapping extensible mouths, these quick flyers gobbled down gnats and midges by the thousands, smaller and larger insects forming a food web cloud above the metal roof of the house. I imagined I could hear audible snaps as dragonfly jaws clamped tight with each mosquito or tiny beetle.

I'm guessing that there were a thousand or more dragonflies in this particular column of air. I tried to imagine the work they were doing for us, providing for free the environmental service of insect population control over Goose Creek—out of whose waters these dragonflies had been born. This presence likely explains why we have no mosquitoes or black flies here.

But then, the next night and the next, only a few dragonflies zipped above the house. And the more I considered it, the more I decided that what I had seen was not locally-hatched dragonflies in such numbers but a swarm of them in a fast-food stop as they migrated through Floyd County, from parts north, bound for who knows where.

Last fall I came upon a group of hawk watchers on the Parkway and for the first time understood from them that some dragonfly species, and only a portion of each population of those species, migrate in the same general directions as the birds of prey. Like the birds, dragonflies ride the winds and even choose the same days as the bird migrants to surge south or rest.

But the spectacle overhead this time of year is not limited to the dragonflies of dusk. Equally as impressive but more demanding that you seek out just exactly the right kind of weather, time of day and kind of light is the procession of the gossamer spiders.

Do let me share with you my account of that amazing vision by reading "Gossamer Days" in *Slow Road Home*, and by all means, see it for yourself in the fall.

Miss the Water: Now
Within Our Means

Sadly, we have not taken the long view of things. We have not been proactive in dealing with problems that extend across borders or beyond administrations. We've used dollars as our sole measure of the health of human economies. We've cast our faith on a repair-shop model in dealing with the things—like our own health—that we knew, sooner or later, we would break if we didn't change our ways.

In a few enlightened instances, we've altered our course slightly, individually and collectively, to address or to apologize for our mistakes, but usually too little, and almost always too late. When it comes to our relationship to the planet, it is by and large a sad legacy of deferred responsibility, nurtured ignorance, haughty indifference and willful inaction that my generation now leaves in the record of our race. But maybe it is not too late for us to change. Maybe we are beginning to know our limits and consider how we might live within them in a sustainable future.

Those limits are not bound, as we've been led to believe, only by the greatness of our vision or ambition or national bank accounts. Ultimately and very soon, we will be constrained by planetary limits, by the finite quantity of life-essential substances that exist within the thin skin of Earth's atmosphere and crust. One of those fixed necessities we will be thinking more about is water.

Less than 1% of the world's fresh water (about 0.007% of all water on earth) is accessible for direct human use. Even so, until mankind's population explosion a few hundred years ago and with the exception of local droughts, there has generally been enough. There will not likely be enough any more. There are far more of us now. Too much good water has gone bad. Worldwide rain distribution patterns are likely to change on a massive scale in our lifetimes, and are doing so even now.

Did you know that Australia is in the midst of a thousand-year drought? Some have said the word "drought" for their situation is too optimistic; it implies a temporary fluctuation. The Aussies may be looking at a very protracted shift in global climate patterns that will keep them very hot and dry for very long.

So the solutions that the island nation devises in the near term may become models for the rest of us for the long haul. With the threat of altered climate patterns ahead, no nation, state or county can count on the past to predict rainfall patterns to come. But one thing for certain: for the planet as a whole, our collective well is quickly running dry.

"The world is incurring a vast water deficit—one that is largely invisible, historically recent, and growing fast. Because much of the deficit comes from aquifer over-pumping, it is often not apparent. Unlike burning forests or invading sand dunes, falling water tables are often discovered only when wells go dry."

-Lester Brown, Emerging Water Shortages.

So what does this have to do with us in Floyd County? To me this coming crisis suggests that now is a good time to miss the water.

At a recent "Green Infrastructure" meeting at the Floyd Country Store, someone asked an expert panelist what was the storage capacity for water in Floyd County's geological structure and how was it likely to hold up to future demands. His answer: nobody knows the answer to that. We just don't have the studies to tell us. He did say that, because of our hard-rock geology, we lack the underground limestone caves and rivers that sustain towns along the I-81 corridor to our north. He noted that in a recent sample of 101 wells, 37 were contaminated by fecal coliform bacteria.

The take-home message is that we need to be thinking in more informed ways about where we site our septic systems. We can do more to treat water as a multi-use resource, utilizing the same rainwater several times and finding ways to send more of it underground to refill our limited fractured-rock reservoirs. We should keep in mind that we get no water from outside our plateau-situated county. We could begin to think of harvesting water in barrels and cisterns and by creating "rain gardens" to keep more of what we get and then use it wisely.

We may soon see that inadequate water for drinking and agriculture leads to starvation and dislocation on an unprecedented global scale. This threat is already looming in places like India and Pakistan where ground water is falling as much as twenty feet per year. In parts of our grain-producing states, the water table has dropped more than 100 feet.

The gold rush for cheap groundwater is almost over. And for all the machinations of regimes and empires, cartels and armies of the world for control of oil, in the end it may be water that we come to see as the most precious liquid of all.

The Parlor Fan Jesus
Not Fish Nor Fowl

Between our pew and the pulpit, two white ceiling fans above the center aisle stirred the humid June air. Beyond the walls the hymnal voices of a few dozen churchgoers lifted to God's ears and those of the few head of cattle that grazed nearby in green pastures beyond the stained glass of Huffville Church. My gaze drifted past the minister's place at the podium to the picture behind him. In six months of Sundays since we starting attending, this was the first time I'd noticed it—a Protestant icon, invisible by virtue of its familiarity.

This same picture (called Heart's Door) I had known in a remarkably similar church of which we once were part—more a part perhaps than any other church we've attended. Our young children gave us a common bond with others, a connection we lack now in our empty-nested years. In the tiny sanctuary of that country church whose property adjoined our little farm in Wythe County hung this very same portrait of a smooth-browed Jesus in radiant robes, dark brown hair rippling over the right shoulder as the figure knocks hopefully at a substantial wooden door tightly shut.

The entryway is symbolically overgrown with thorny, unpruned roses of our sinful lives. The door conspicuously lacks an outside latch so only the soul within can open it. And if anyone within will only answer...

I closed my eyes and the picture on the wall transported me farther back still as the Huffville minister ministered on. And there it was in every detail—the same white robe and beatific demeanor more than a half-century ago. I remembered asking my mother "Is that really Jesus?"

When she explained that there were no photographs from Christ's day, I wondered how somebody could just make up the face of God. Until yesterday at the computer after church, I knew nothing more about this oh-so-common "portrait" of the faith, an image that for millions has become the face of the real, historical Jesus.

The painting is the work of Warner E. Sallman. He created a charcoal sketch in 1924 that he called The Son of Man and from that produced a color painting, The Head of Christ, in 1940. His Jesus was a kinder, gentler Presence than the more austere divine countenance imagined by his Victorian artist predecessors. Sallman's Christ was immediately popular, accessible and reassuring in a very troubled time. Many a wallet sized image went to war. In peace and war since then, with more than 500 million reproductions, that same Jesus image and its spin-offs have become an industry of sorts.

This face of a European-looking sepia-toned Christ found on everything from calendars to tongue-depressor-handled church pew fans has not been without its detractors, seen by some as too effeminate. This visage was once displayed side by side with a shampoo advertisement comparing the holy coif with that of the famous Breck Girl. The lighting and backdrop does give the bust a look as if it might have been taken in an Olin Mills studio in Anywhere, USA—a familiarity that I suppose puts us at once at ease.

Has the Good Shepherd been marketed and commodified? Perhaps. But we will of necessity conjure images for those in our hearts and minds. And it seems likely that no single depiction of God has unified the imaginings of so many believers in my lifetime on a single face—believers who, when they have a friend in Jesus, walk and talk in their gardens alone with the very same bronzed and bearded personage I saw today behind the pulpit once again, for the first time.

Fast Roads of FLoyd
Local Color

Inasmuch as we experience distant places, by and large, on wheels rather than on foot, the character of roads (and the view from them, the fellow-travelers on them) contributes in no small degree to the impression we carry home of what those other places are like.

Or so I mused one July day as I drove Daniels Run from Goose Creek to Christiansburg. Just about the time I reached the crest near Gearhart's Garage, I wondered: how do Floyd County roads reflect the character of its people and community and place? What do our byways tell about natural topography and those who traverse it? If my sudden speculation here was true that we are shaped by the roads we drive and how we drive them, then who are we?

You may have visited places in other parts of the country where the land is flat and the roads are arrow-straight. They run monotonously true north-south or east-west and meet at perfect 90 degree crossings. Except for the occasional jack rabbit or mule deer, there isn't much to watch out for on such roads—no sudden hairpin curves, no sharp drop-off shoulders into creeks or rivers, no goat-worthy vertical rises to climb, or to descend in low gear down the other side. Straight and level roads in such flat places are inherently fast roads. Ours are, by nature, decidedly slow.

By that point in my travels and musings, Daniels Run had become High Rock Hill Road which wiggled through the mountain ridges and was about to become South Franklin. From the bridge over I-81 I could see an unbroken line of eighteen-wheelers disappeared to the vanishing point east and west along the corridor of travel through the Ridge and Valley. America's efficient bee-lines of motorized commerce have taken that same buffalo-path of least resistance through valleys in impassable sandstone mountains that the earliest settlers chose when heading for Kentucky and parts west.

It seems likely that no wagon trains two hundred years ago chose to route their westward journey through Floyd County. Our roads even today are not designed for speed. They ease along the topographic contours of ancient quartz-and-granite mountains. Here, geology sets the course of commerce and rate of travel rather than the earth-moving heavy hand that removes mountains to suit the road builder's sense of efficiency and speed. Consequently, the roads of Floyd County are necessarily slow. Some are slower than others.

In less that two miles between our house and the hardtop, a driver will come upon eleven blind approaches. The road rises and bends when the creek does. The creek bends and falls when the rock of the mountain allows it. Five miles an hour is the safe speed as you near a blind gravel single-lane curve where the edge of the road is also the lip of a ravine. It doesn't pay to be in a hurry on our slow road. So we try to adapt our schedule to the roads we travel rather than impose our hurry on a mountain path that is slow by nature of landscape. We hope that others on our road will do the same, but experience tells me otherwise.

Too many times in the past several months, the speed limit (established for dry roads in good visibility without deer) is not fast enough for the car behind me. And woe is me should I slow down around a bend to actually see the forest or the roadside wildflowers as anything more than a blur of color, light and shadow zipping past my window.

So contrary to my contrary nature, I pull over and let the driven individual drive far too fast for the road or their own or their neighbor's good to "save" a few precious minutes in their hurried lives.

My very opinionated observation is that speeds are creeping up in our county, even as traffic volume increases. And I wonder if there is any way to teach our children as well as our visiting tourists the importance of slowing down inside the county, and not just for reasons of safety.

It bears saying again: the slower you go, the more you see. The more you see, the more you know of your place in this world. The more you know, the more you care about and care for.

The landscape of the Blue Ridge has a special character, a resonant energy and quality that is best appreciated, I think, on foot. But knowing most visitors will come here and pass through on wheels, let it be known that to know the land they travel through, to partake of the qualities that make this place special and different from flat, straight and efficient travel of busier places, on our roads, slower is better.

Closer to the Bone
Body and Soul Together

I've been resisting, but push (that'd be the wife) is coming to shove (that's me) and we may be keeping chickens again by springtime. Why bother? Because we can, and because we really should—the former is easier to explain.

Our neighbor down the road is making and selling hen houses that are well built, far more secure against chick-and-egg varmints than our barn, and more or less portable for free-range relocation around our pasture. So there's the how of the poultry enterprise: the task is relatively easily do-able, accessible and affordable.

But the moral and ethical imperatives that lead us toward backyard poultry have to do with bigger issues: eating locally, eating lower on the food chain, and as a matter of personal responsibility.

We like the idea of eating locally-grown meat. We've been willing to drive from the eastern to the western ends of the county to get it. But the time-energy-carbon costs are just too high to keep this up. So if we could convert our sunlight and pasture into protein without the drive to Willis, that makes sense.

That we (all of us carnivores) should eat less meat and more locally grown fruits and vegetables is not up for debate in today's world. The cost in required water, land and energy to produce a pound of beef versus a pound of grain are easy enough to compare, and difficult to ignore in a crowded world. The health impact of too much animal fat in the diet of an obese nation is also an inconvenient truth in the discussion of shoulds and oughts.

Yet globally, far too many humans have too little, and baby brains grown with inadequate protein don't fare so well. To feed the world's population of 6.7 billion (July 2008 figure), we will need to change both our dietary preferences towards less red meat per capita and our methods of obtaining animal protein overall. (The discussion of more humane husbandry and especially of how many humans is too many for sustainability certainly need to enter the global conversation very soon.)

Add to these thorny issues the fact that, as America (123 kg per person per year meat consumption) and Europe are recognizing the need to eat less meat, those who have never until now been able to afford much meat want much more if it in their diets (read: China, India—5 kg per person per year—and Indonesia). The Big Mac attack is going global; Amazonian rain forests are being converted to pastures to grow more Beijing Burgers.

The solutions to this serious environmental and vexing personal conundrum, present and future, range from the sublime and simple (the path that Push and Shove are looking for) to the more far-fetched high-tech options. Some are seriously advocating that insects and other invertebrates provide a certain portion of the protein in our diet. I'm thinking nightcrawlers might be tasty with those fresh eggs we'll be gathering come spring.

Even more Star-Trekian, "meat without feet" can be grown in laboratory vats using the same tissue culture methods that makes new skin for burn victims. I'm not making this up (as Dave Barry used to be fond of saying). And with so much meat with feet treading the planet in our day, it makes me think that Solyent Green (1973, starring Charlton Heston) might be worth watching again.

Beef and pork cooperatives seem ripe to happen in communities like ours where one family has the fenced pasture; another can do the butchering. Several families share and the small, well cared-for, grass-fed, chemical-free meat that is enjoyed in small portions from time to time rather than being the central item in every meal. (How much? MyPyramid.gov recommends 5.5 oz of meat and beans in a daily 2000 calorie diet.)

So I suppose my wife is right: having our own source for eggs and meat fits nicely with our efforts to grow more of our own vegetables. And working harder for our protein, we'll settle for meat as a treat, not a habitual entitlement. And our hearts and blood vessels—and the planet—will be better off for the effort.

Time Machine
For the Time, Being

One summer not long after college, a good friend and I were backpacking through the sunken canyons of the Bankhead Wilderness in north Alabama.

We laid out our sleeping bags that afternoon in the humid shade under a massive ledge of sandstone. From there we looked out on the Sipsey River close below us. A summer shower sent sheets of warm rain sweeping over the narrow swath of forest between rocky rims. The sound of it hissed softly like the surf in a seashell.

Lying on my back with my hands clasped behind my head, a serene and wordless hour passed between us. I blinked away a speck of sand, and then another. A few minutes later, my friend reached up and wiped at his eyes. He turned to me with an amused chuckle in an instant of mutual comprehension. In that twinkling, we grasped the cosmic scale of single grains of sand falling from the massive roof of our seemingly immutable stone shelter.

So this is what becomes of mountains, we said, and laughed, the irony of the moment understood.

Later that afternoon, we sat on a ferny boulder above the river. Deep in its warm green waters small fish held their place, barely, against the current.

"They use up a lot of energy just to keep from being swept to the sea," I remarked.

"We all do, Fred. We all do" my friend said.

And as we sat quietly watching, listening, the sandy bottom of mountain bits beneath those bright fish washed, speck by grain and foot by foot, towards a distant Gulf Coast beach.

From A High Place
Within These Walls

I wrote this hours after the experience, back before the days I wrote with any regularity or purpose. It was only a few months after we'd moved into this old house and we were still pretty puffed up by the heady fact that we now owned the paradise that we'd dreamed of all our lives. Before including this here, I had only shared this very personal account with a few. It was always one of my mom's favorites, and it is for her that I've added it.

I grew up in a time and place where the daily recitation of the pledge, a poem, and a psalm was a somber but essential beginning to each school day. My sixth grade classmates and I would stand beside our desks, our voices droning in unison through the morning ritual. I can still recite most of it, more than 40 years later. We started by speaking to the flag, hands across our hearts. We always ended the liturgy with the 121st Psalm, speaking to God. "I will lift up mine eyes unto the hills, from whence cometh my help." I have never forgotten it. I think of it frequently, since I have been called to live in a land of hills.

With each step, the psalm repeated like a mantra that day, breathing in, breathing out. I climbed with effort, conscious of working against gravity's resistance. Every couple of steps, when I could look up briefly from my erratic path through the rough mountainside underfoot, I lifted my eyes on the diagonal, toward my destination at the crest of the steepest part of the highest ridge on our land. It sits at the end of our valley, where steep ridges join like the arms of a letter Y to form a sort of gorge. This cleft is in the center of my view as I sit at my desk, prominent as I look from the steps of the front porch. But I had never been on that ridgetop, and I had not intended to go there on this particular day.

We bought the farm in Floyd County almost a year ago, but had only enjoyed actually living here for four months on the day I tell you about. For a year before that, our time and energies had been focused on making the old farmhouse livable. But today the work for a while at least was past, and I was climbing a mountain, my mountain, tracing the limits of our domain, exploring, being led to a place I had never been on my own land.

I had left the house only intending to carry a couple of buckets over to the barn, intending to come on back to the warm house before the cold rains came in. But at the barn, to my surprise, I dropped my work gloves and my jacket and set off walking up the logging road toward the south end of the valley. "The Heart has reasons which Reason cannot know," said Pascal.

Maybe I was following my heart for reasons I might someday learn. I left our usual gentle path and struck off against the contours, roughly following our boundary almost vertically up into the rhododendrons. This was not a rational course, as anyone understands who has ever attempted to steer a straight path up a steep slope through a laurel thicket. After struggling hand over fist for thirty feet, I was surprised and relieved to discover a hidden deer path under the canopy of the arching shrubs.

Even on a trail, the stepping over fallen trunks and ducking under tangles of rhododendron was very much like work. I needed a breathing break every dozen paces. There were times in my thirties and forties when I would have just tromped right to the top without a rest, I thought to myself. But today, and truly for the last several months, I had been more aware of gravity's increasing demands on my energies. I frequently half-jokingly have said that, when gardening season comes around again every year, the ground has gotten farther down than it was the year before. And I was sure that this hill was steeper than it was the year before, but not as steep as it will be next year.

I was proud of myself and pleased to be there, halfway up the slope, with a reasonable reserve of energy left and a heart rate that was significant but not dangerous. I took off my sweatshirt and tied it around my waist. I felt robust and alive, a little tired and certain my face was flushed with the exertion.

Bent over, my hands braced on my knees, I breathed hard at one of my rest stops. Looking over, still bent, twenty feet in front of me stood an old chestnut fence post and the remnants of a few rails, mostly gone to leaf mold. Farther up the steep slope, another piece of a post pushed up barely above the forest floor. So, this must be our southern property line. As I walked a little higher, near the crest of the next hill beyond a shallow saddle, I found the remnants of a very old and formerly very active sawmill, with logging waste piled twenty feet high. So I am not the first to come here, I thought.

Through the bare branches of the oaks and pines, I was by then high enough to see over the tops of the Rhododendrons, to the distant ridges, and down the long valley back toward the clearing by our barn. A dozen more paces higher, our farmhouse came into view. With a rush of joy and pride, I admired the beauty of a panorama where nearly everything I could see was mine. I had overcome tangled branches, loose rock, steep slopes and rational reluctance to get here. The day belonged to me. I felt like nobility!

From a moss-covered rock, I soaked up the moment, sitting with my sweaty back against a slanting chestnut oak. The sun broke through the thickening gray clouds, briefly casting a shaft of golden light down the valley. Cloud shadows raced up from the meadow and over the hilltop. In the distance, four large deer trudged slowly and unconcerned up the logging road on our eastern ridge. Just then, a flock of Canada geese flew honking in formation directly overhead, passed directly over our new home, then vanished over the northern horizon.

This was almost too much. I sat in awe, exhilarated and puzzled. Is this why I was led to this place at this time, on an unexpected and illogical excursion up a hidden trail: to have a Kodak moment? To gloat from a pinnacle, master of all I surveyed? What did this mean, what lesson was I to learn?

The storm gathered, a few drops of rain fell. But I knew I should wait here a while longer for an insight that seemed almost in reach. I do not as a rule and did not that afternoon hear God's audible voice, and what I came away with did not come to me as one uninterrupted, divine, soliloquy. Even so, I was granted my insight that day, and was able to write down these words not long after I returned home:

"Yes, I brought you to this high place. I am pleased to have you enjoy this small piece of Earth that you call yours. You have already told me that you under-stand that you are merely the steward of this patch of forest and field."

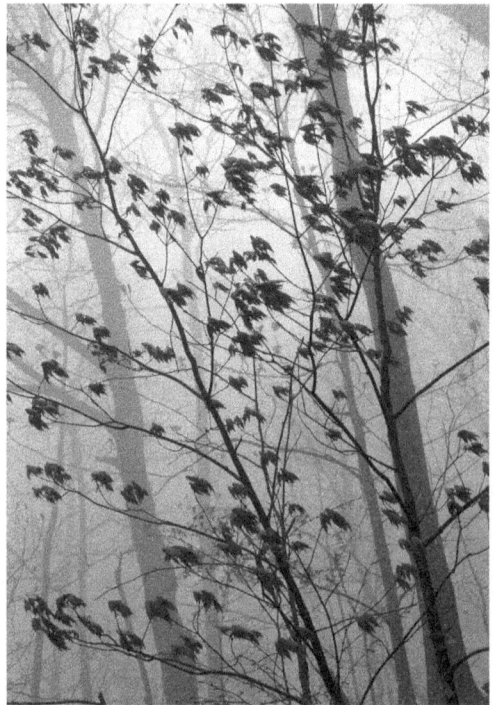

"Be happy that you can share this place with others, but know you are not the only humans who have known or will enjoy the beauty here. Ownership may have meaning and purpose in your system of law, but you do not own this land any more than you own the air you have struggled for today or the sunlight that falls upon your face now. I gladly give it to you. You take it in, use it, draw energy and life from it, and it all comes back."

"You have your sense of the beautiful because I made you that way. You understand that this resonance with The Good is one of the ways in which you are created in my image."

"These special moments I give you are testaments of my love for you. They are not ends in themselves. The beauty that you find in nature, hear in music, and know in reason are aspects of my creative nature, good and perfect gifts that are intimations of my ultimate Plan for you and for mankind. Be patient, be still and know this."

"You have known my Presence today on this hill which you can see from all corners of this parcel of Earth for the remainder of your days. You will seldom return here, but this place will survive you by many years. Your children's children will visit me in this place and know what you have known here."

I sat there for a while longer, rested and content, knowing now why I had struggled up to that peak on that hour. The winds picked up and the air grew sharply cooler. I wrapped my sweatshirt across my shoulders and rose stiffly to head back to the house. Looking down from the end of the ridge so high above our gravel road and home, I prepared my mind to enter again into the tasks of the day that I had abandoned for my encounter on the hill. I stopped by the barn to get my gloves and jacket. It was beginning to rain in big, heavy drops.

A few pieces of dry kindling quickly brought the fire to life, flickering amber light through the glass doors of the wood stove. With the warmth, I grew drowsy. My legs ached some and my back was tired. I sank into the couch, content to be still.

Turning to look out the window, up the valley, south, to the top of the hill, I thought again of the Psalm. And I said aloud "The Lord shall preserve my going out and my coming in...also my going up, and my coming down... from this time forth, and even forevermore." And I fell fast asleep.

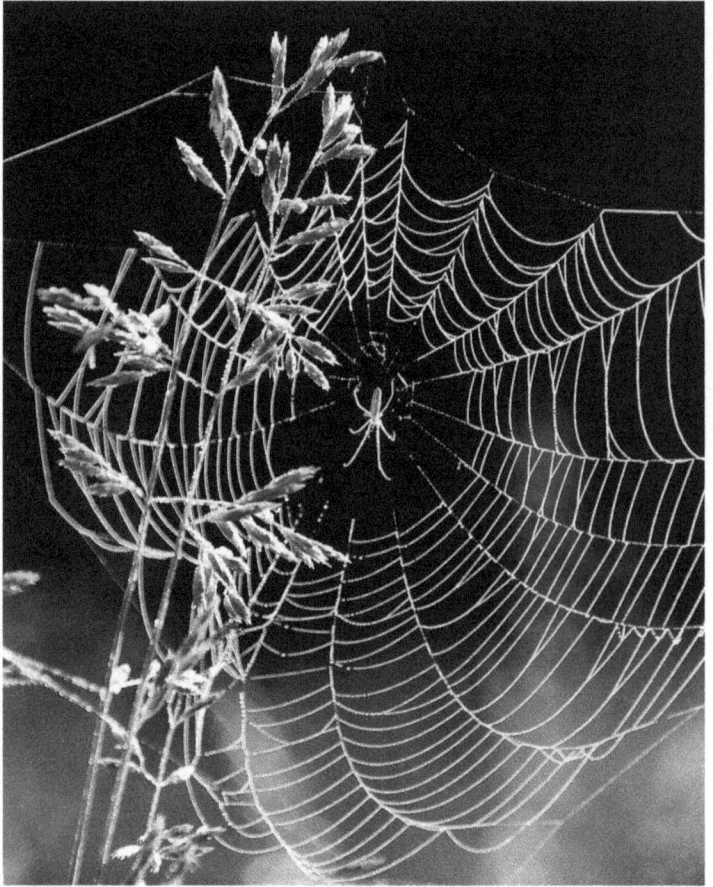

And in wonder, it has been said, is the beginning of wisdom.

3

A Necessary Nutrient of Childhood
Curious By Nature

The Badlands appeared ten thousand feet beneath the plane a few jet-minutes before we touched down in Rapid City, I envied the pilot's cockpit view: the jagged Needles of the South Dakota Black Hills north of town, and south, the high dome of buffalo-browsed Custer State Park. Presidential visages of Mt. Rushmore stood in rocky relief not twenty miles from my daughter's house. What a wild kingdom our newborn grand daughter Taryn and her six year old sister Abby might come to know here, I thought, even while lamenting how far away from us they live.

Fifteen minutes after landing, we turned into the driveway of our daughter's hill-side suburban home. Since we had been out in May, they'd had some landscaping done. The front yard was orderly, trimmed and tamed. The back was fenced now, the standard green quarter-acre rectangle with the obligatory swing set sporting in smooth plastic trim what passes these days for a tree house—with no tree.

I had hoped at least for some pictures of Abby playing on her swings while we were in town, but it didn't take long to discover that, like so many suburban kids, she spends most of her play time indoors. In her safe, manicured back yard, no rough edges challenge her muscles or entice her curiosity and imagination. No unknowns invite her to explore and discover in the way they do when she creates her own play for entire afternoons here on Goose Creek on visits once or twice a year.

How sad, I thought. Our grand daughter living so close to wilderness doesn't experience wildness near home, a freedom that at her age, I needed and found at the edges of a Birmingham neighborhood long ago. Looking back, I see how very important those secret places were for knitting in me and others a connection and attachment to the natural world. Early exposure to those tiny, secret microcosms of the greater landscape became the seed-beds of belonging to the place and planet where we lived, and so many of today's children never know them at all.

I'm talking here about patches that were no larger—and in many cases much smaller—than our grand daughters' back yard. For me it was a wooded vacant lot on the cul-de-sac; a tangled bank on the edge of the grammar school property; the hedgerow at our uncle's house; and the pond where my mother took me to fish—and more often than not, I abandoned my pole and explored the muddy banks instead.

But those half-acre childhood wilds are harder to find these days, and they have become less permissible places to play on one's own. Unvisited, they no longer seem necessary or magic or special in the way they were for me and my friends. Today's children play indoors. They are taxied to and from team sports in the SUV. The children are safe, barricaded in their fortress-homes.

While dinner cooked, Abby and I played "hide the croquet ball" among the new foundation plantings. Beside the house, angular, crushed native stone mulched the junipers. We sat down and began to turn the shards of rock, looking at the sparkly flecks in the granite, choosing out the waxy-translucent pieces of quartz into a separate pile.

"Abby, did you know that every one of these little rocks was once part of a mountain?" She was amazed to know this, thinking rocks had always been rocks. Sitting tailor-fashion in the shade, we talked about how the mountains had pushed up, and over time, worn away. We talked about sand and soil, about plants and erosion and rivers and beaches.

I mentioned how a rock tumbler could do to these rough stones what the abrasion of water had done over time, making them smooth, polished and like jewels. Abby reminded me of this machinery a dozen times before we left to return to Virginia. Could she have a rock tumbler? I think I know now what the maternal grandfather will be sending the girls for Christmas this year.

Meanwhile, back home to Floyd County once again, parks are being created in the downtown area. Trail systems are coming together across the county. Farm land and woodlands are being preserved in conservation easements. And thankfully, many Floyd County boys and girls still have the possibility of acceptably safe, rough edges in which to grow their confidence and imaginations, their muscles and sense of kinship with the natural world.

Many of our American historical figures who have held the land in high esteem relate their early visions of connectedness to earth and society back to their young years. Hidden in a private sanctuary of shrubs just beyond the edge of things, reading and pretending in tree houses, building forts in the woods, chasing frogs beside a farm pond. They could imagine in the clouds the shape of the future.

Allow and encourage your young children and grand children to enjoy their personal wild kingdoms near home. Show them the way. This legacy you bestow may go on and on, so that a half-dozen generations from now, a little girl who looks a little like you will chose to make her own bow-and-arrow in the woods rather than spend an afternoon shopping for new headphones at the Sky Mall.

Floyd County's Alien Invaders
Earth Companions

Aliens haunt my childhood memories. They could be spooky, but even so, my friends and I created caves and tunnels through tendril webs of these exotic life forms. They came from a world away, creatures that settled in for good on our street, in our back yard, looming and sinister against the skyline. It wasn't ET or unearthly War of the Worlds monsters that haunted our neighborhood, but the green invader infamous even then for conquering places it didn't belong—kudzu, the rampant runaway weed of the south.

Kudzu's infamy lies in its remarkable rate of growth and tolerance of growing conditions. I've heard that the only effective mulch for kudzu is the concrete block, and that the best fertilizer is waste 10W40 motor oil. This exaggeration says a lot about invasive plants in general: they tend to grow aggressively under the harshest of conditions to the detriment of native plants. They have few enemies to keep them in check.

This vine was imported from Japan in 1876 to stabilize steep road banks and ostensibly, to provide forage for cattle. Cattle do love it, but not as much as the cancerous vine loves the red clay soil of Alabama and Georgia. (It's range is creeping north as winters become warmer.) Even though the plant, a bean relative, is high in nutrition, cattle can't keep it in control, especially after it reaches the highest branches of every tree in its path, and climbs out on power lines that provide safe passage for kudzu's spread to the other side of the highway, and to the next yard and the town beyond.

An "invasive" by definition is a plant or animal species that has been introduced (not uncommonly by human action or intention) to a place where it did not previously occur naturally (i.e., is not native). There it becomes capable of establishing a breeding population in the new location without further intervention by humans. In its new location, it becomes a pest, threatening the local biodiversity. And let me tell you, it isn't necessary to go to Alabama to find invasives.

Floyd County has its own share and the list is growing. This matter of not-from-around-here plants and animals taking over the local landscape has been a biology pet-issue of mine for years, but it reached a new level of alarm with a recent visit to the Blue Ridge Parkway back in October.

I once drove this particular stretch of parkway almost every day and came to know it well. So the fact that an Asian invasive called Tree of Heaven (Ailanthus) dominates the treescape along the parkway did not surprise me. What did shock me in my October visit was that, in the couple of years since we've moved from that side of the county, the trees and bushes along this stretch of roadway have been "kudzu-ed" by yet another Asian invader: Oriental Bittersweet.

"Oriental bittersweet is an aggressive invader that threatens all vegetation levels of forested and open areas. It grows over other vegetation, completely covering it, and kills other plants by preventing photosynthesis, girdling, and uprooting by force of its massive weight." (Find on the web, Weeds Gone Wild: Alien Plant Invaders of Natural Areas.)

The Department of Conservation and Recreation lists other highly-aggressive Virginia invasive plants that include multiflora rose, Canada thistle, garlic mustard, autumn olive, wineberry, Japanese honeysuckle, Chinese privet and many more species that grow faster and more aggressively than species you may prefer in your yard, pasture and forest. Do you know these plants?

Animals, too, can be invaders—flying, swimming, slithering or carried by plane, train or automobile to where they have never lived before. Consider as an example the European Starling, no one's favorite bird. The species was successfully imported to Central Park in the 1890s under the misguided romantic notion that it would be lovely to have all the birds mentioned anywhere in Shakespeare's plays. Abducted over a distance from its habitat of origin where it was in balance with natural predators and such, the starling is now said to be the most abundant bird in the world—a serious agricultural pest and a nuisance in cities on every continent.

But what is the so-what? Is this only an issue of concern for taxonomists and biological purists? Maybe non-natives are simply 'weedy' plants and animals free-loading in places they didn't originally come from, and no matter; or could there be larger consequences from the homogenization of the world's creatures? If this invasion continues, there will someday before long be no such a thing as "native" plants and animals. And that loss of the unique plants and animals that make here unique from there will be for some of us as terrible a tragedy as the strip-mall sameness that other invasives have brought to our towns and counties.

And I should tell you that the week I found Oriental bittersweet along the Parkway, I also discovered it haunting the edge of the local library parking lot.

Company is Coming: Resistance is Futile
Earth Companions

In these cooler days of autumn, while we look forward to bringing our lives indoors to the comfort of our warm homes, thousands upon thousand of house guests are planning to visit us. Even now they are packing their tiny bags and heading home to your place for the winter and you might as well know them by name.

They are called the Multicolored Asian Lady Beetle or MALB for short. Highly variable in their color and number of spots, they are also sometimes referred to as Halloween Beetles or Harlequin Lady Beetles, or in our house simply, the (expletive deleted) Ladybugs.

In October, being no respecter of persons, swarming masses of Harmonia axyridis descend upon the godly and the ungodly, the air tight and the loosely constructed alike. You will within the month have a house full of these little stinkers, so steel yourselves, good neighbors.

When will they come? Most likely on the second day after temperatures are greater the 65 degrees just following a dramatic drop in temperature, usually to near freezing. So. You were warned.

In one study, the average type of house experiencing an MALB infestation problem was 73 years old, two-story, wood or vinyl sided and it had lots of trees on at least three sides of the house. Hello. That's where I live exactly!

Heck of it is, these critters don't belong in this country at all. Like the infernal Starling and irrepressible Kudzu, they too were brought here on purpose, if you can believe that! Considerable uncertainty lies in exactly who is to blame and precisely when, as there have been many intentional and accidental releases going back to at least 1916.

Only in the last 15 (generally warmer) years or so have these insects managed to survive and spread, and in so doing, they have produced some success toward their original and intended purpose: to control aphids in agricultural and land-scape environments. But they also out-feed and even gobble up other native lady beetles. So once again, nature gives with one hand, and takes away with the other, and significantly in the "take" column, your walls and mine will soon be crawling with orange and black spots.

In our first encounter with them en masse was in 1999 as we restored our old house on Goose Creek. I quickly learned that swatting these crawling freckles as they huddled in the corners on the south and west walls was NOT the control measure of choice. Like all lady beetles, when startled or agitated, they "reflex-bleed" an odiferous yellow-staining fluid from their leg joints. However, the "blood" of the MALBs contains a much higher concentration of the off-putting defense chemical than most lady beetles. They swarm. They bite. They stink. What's not to love?

So our removal method of choice is to suck them up with the wand of the vacuum cleaner. Out loud, I tally each one with some satisfaction as the number rises and each one disappears into the nozzle. I take no small pleasure in seeing a few hundred of them contained finally inside the clear canister. I suggest other fates than capture and release.

The fellow who painted this old place for us was the first to tell me that these polka-dotted insects could inflict pain (as he swatted them with a wet paint-brush!) They don't bite in a defensive sort of way, but they are inclined to sample the back of your neck just in case you might be some mutant kind of aphid, and therefore edible. I understand that about 30% of house-dwelling MALBs are inclined to bite, and on the hands of certain college-student volun-teers, they continued to chew for up to 30 minutes!

Fortunately, these multicolored beetles don't carry any disease organisms, so far as I can find. However, like their distant relatives the mites, a person can develop an allergic reaction to their inhaled "dust" once it is ground up to a fine powder in your carpets. This can result in a kind of eye irritation as well as an asthma-like condition—injury to insult.

And finally, I have a personal theory about MALB that I'll share with you, and it is this: they come into existence by spontaneous generation. Vacuum ten of them out of the corner of the window; look away briefly, and presto! Five more have appeared at the very edge of your peripheral vision and out of thin air! Likewise, while their little corpses accumulate all over your carpet, you'll never see one actually in the act of falling. Except…

A favorite winter pass-time: watch for the heat from the wood stove to overcome an over-flying MALB. It falls down on the hot metal stove, flips immediately over onto its rounded back and does a little spinning break-dance sort of thing as it extends its underwings and gives up the ghost.

On the short, bleak days of mid-winter, this will be about the most exciting thing happening in this old house in the hinterlands We have to take our entertainment where we find it.

Mt. Rogers Remembered
Within Our Means

This year, the 34th annual Mt. Rogers Naturalist Rally happens in May and I will go. It will be like going home. But then again, neither I nor the world is the same as it was the first time I gathered with others for the Saturday morning field trips at Konnarock.

It was the spring of 1976 and as a young faculty member, I'd successfully petitioned the community college to let me offer a new plant life course that I would gladly develop—a class I envisioned as field trip intensive, wild foods and ecology-minded, hands-on

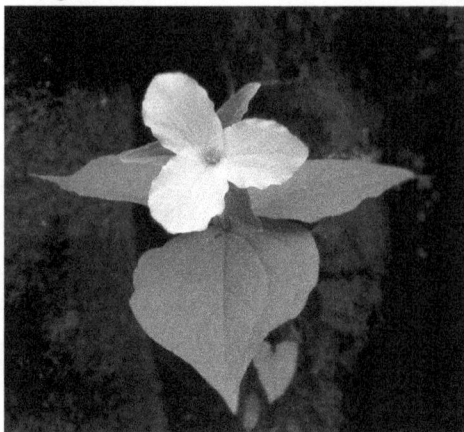

botany. The class was offered, and students (from local freshmen to retired world travelers) signed up. We began our field excursions right away in a small caravan out to stalk the wild asparagus!

I was told about a new outdoor event in May at Mt. Rogers and was intrigued: a congregation of fellow tree huggers! Ten students went with me to the event; we pitched our tents Friday night after the dinner and speaker and awoke at daylight to a light frost.

Saturday morning, more than 120 participants gathered to be matched with the designated field trip leader of a dozen scheduled events—birds, plants, geology, small mammals, mosses, salamanders and more. But one of the leaders had become ill at the last minute. Could anybody lead a wildflower field trip, the organizers asked from the top of the steps of the old hemlock-bark-sided CCC building?

My students pushed me toward the front and I reluctantly agreed. It was such a rewarding experience that I went back for eleven years to lead the same field trip over the same familiar terrain. Grindstone's nature trail crosses the gentle slopes of rich cove forest—a 3/4 mile loop where year after year I repeated my little speechlets at the same bends of the trail about this fern or lichen or wildflower. I came to know the place by heart.

In 1987 we moved away, and not long after returning to Virginia in 1997, I revisited Grindstone and the Naturalist Rally—a kind of double homecoming. Many of the human faces were the same, save for the passage of time. Some folks in my long absence had never missed a single year. But much about the natural face of the area was not the same, even in the short span of years since I first came to know the area in 1976.

The dark visage of the area's 5000-foot mountain crests (Rogers, Whitetop and Pine) are less dark now than they were then. The evergreens (spruce-fir, white pine and eastern Hemlock) are under siege by adelgids and beetles and the trees' ability to resist is compromised by acid precipitation and climate change. The summit trails are strewn with unnatural blow-down of dead treetops, open light reaching the mossy forest floor that was for centuries in dark shade all day long.

The birders at Mt. Rogers see a different mix of birds now on their field trip, some species less abundant, others missing entirely, many showing up at odd times as the northern migration season warms earlier than what has long been normal. The accelerating disappearance of tropical forest converted over the past four decades to pasture for beef production, and now to biofuel crops spells doom for many once-familiar Virginia summer songbirds that winter in shrinking South American habitat.

And saddest of all for me: on my solo reunion walk around Whispering Waters trail at Grindstone in 1998, some of my old friends—rose twisted stalk, showy orchis, umbrella-leaf, and yellow trillium—were not there where I had always found them all those May field trips before.

I want to stick my finger in the dike, to click my heels and have the natural order right again. Can humankind live in harmony with this world for good? Can we as good stewards keep an eye on the sparrow even while we live off the bounty of our finite home place?

If in the end it turns out that we can successfully be both stewards and consumers of our vanishing natural wealth, such a change of heart and habit will come in no small measure from those across the world who live in or find it often essential to visit nature, those who are attuned to its nuances and small wonders and who by necessity or choice, immerse themselves in the outdoors—many for the sheer love of it.

So I'll be pleased to cast my lot again this year with the bird-watching, stream stalking, butterfly-netting, tree-hugging naturalists at Mt. Rogers—a group who, as a whole, are filled with wonder in the out-of-doors. And in wonder, it has been said, is the beginning of wisdom.

A Writer is a Hunter Who Tastes Life Twice
Not Fish Nor Fowl

For almost three years now, writing has been as regular a morning habit as drinking (too much) coffee. And I should tell you: the practice began in a blog. No, that's not a muddy depression full of cattails and sedges. A "web-log" or blog is a medium of internet self-publishing that is ridiculously simple to create: type something with your keyboard, hit "publish" and literally any net-connected person in the world can instantly become your reader.

I'm an unabashed cheerleader for the blog as a legitimate, worthwhile medium for writing of all kinds and am convinced it is more than a passing fad. I wanted to talk more about writing in general—and your writing, in particular.

Aren't you a writer? I have reached the point where I am able to say that "I am a writer" without feeling like a complete imposter, but only because I think of it in this way: one who hunts—even if he carries his gun into the woods and comes home with nothing—is still called a hunter. So in this way, I am a writer. The daily weblog (Fragments from Floyd) confirms I take those daily walks, hunting (with more or less success) for the right words to tell whatever story it is that comes to mind or heart. Many of you are writers, too, but have not yet joined the hunt.

To be a writer simply means that you transform your inner life, your senses or experiences into words. To become an earnest writer, someone has said you must "write every day; write from the heart; write what you know." There is nothing more to it than that, even if, in our hunt, we often fire and miss.

But then most word-hunters don't write because they are certain of bagging game and a very few are certain of pay for their words. After all, necessity, ego or mere ambition make for an ugly muse. Few of us write for a living; but writing as a discipline can certainly make our living richer.

But what could you possibly write about, you want to know—just as I did several years ago, facing the blank screen of the blog each morning. People are naturally interested in the unique, personal accounts of others. Just look at the popularity of "reality" TV. (No, on second thought, don't look.)

We all have it in us to be writers because we each have a unique story to tell. We may not all be bouncy-bouncy fun-fun-fun, but like Tigger, each of us is the only one! Personal weblogs have given would-be word-gatherers like me a purpose, an accountability and an audience for our stories—even when they come from adventures no further abroad than our own back yards, streets of town, or family gatherings.

The fragments of daily life that we may record in words—about our dogs or children, our creeks or forests, our gardens and travel through the stages of life—each show, for better or worse, some small truth about our unique place and purpose in this world. Taken together, the trivial threads—memories, insights, hopes realized or lost—weave the fabric of our stories. This is what we hold in our hands; we know it well and can write about it from the heart.

Beauty, humor and meaning hover invisible around us. The words we find in our hunt make those good things visible, give them shape and color, and encourage us to pay closer attention to the ordinary. For a vigilant writer, there is no ordinary. I encourage you to take up your pen or keyboard and begin to write. You'll not know what you think until you see what you say. And you might just be surprised at what you discover when you step outside your door, hunting for words.

Shaped by Place
Local Color

Bear with me in this thought exercise and lament about the seemingly irreconcilable good ends of progress and of preservation. It was written after I saw a shopping mall had replaced a favorite boyhood mountaintop wilderness in my hometown.

It is the year 1809. I am a Scots-Irish immigrant seeking independence and a few hundred acres of wilderness to farm, so that I might carry on the traditions of my ancestors in the expanding society of America. I hold here a handbill stating that there is cheap land available in far western Virginia, along the New River. And everything I will do and everywhere I will go and how I will get where I am going—all of my future is determined by the lay of that land.

The pitch and grade of the primitive trail determines where I can and cannot go as I move generally westward. The roadway, such as it is, limits the size and weight of my wagon, and thus, the belongings I can bring with me. The weather and season effects when my animals can find browse, when dry paths will allow travel, when I must seek shelter or die.

My destination of three hundred acres of my choosing on the newly acquired Indian lands will be determined by the character of the place: will I and my animals find water there? How does the land suit for crops, and is it level enough so my oxen can clear the forest? Is the soil rich and deep? Will the staples that I cannot make or produce myself come from a nearby settlement?

From day to day, once I arrive and over the years make my home, my life and livelihood will be determined by the nature of the landscape: I must have a lover's knowledge of every fold and hillock and holler around me, because it is from this physical place that I kill game for food, find herbs for medicine, select just the right kind of wood for the tools I craft in order to survive. Place determines whether I live or die, and I respect it's limitations, honor it's provision and will spend a lifetime living in an uneasy balance with it, seeking to understand it thoroughly.

It is the year 2009. I am the direct descendent of the settler from two hundred years ago. I live near where my ancestors settled in Southwest Virginia. His notions of dependence on the providence of place is foreign to me, primal and repugnant.

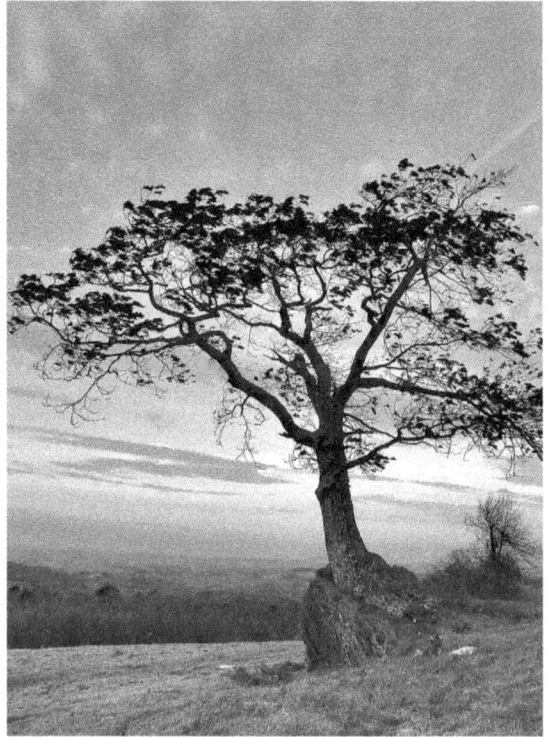

To assume that place shapes us and constrains us in any way is to acknowledge that there are forces or conditions imposed on us by our physical surroundings. This is a limiting and archaic way of thinking in our modern age of freedom from the effects of place upon people. In my day, place is merely an object of action and its givens are only temporary impediments to progress. The places my great, great, great grandfather knew are being tamed, transmuted, altered by our living here as we deem best. This is the modern way of thinking about place.

If there is a mountain where we want a shopping plaza, we take it down. If there is a stream where we want a road, we divert it into the dark of underground pipes. We modify and control every aspect about where we live—our microclimate, the ubiquitous ambient noises, the texture and color and order of everything from our clothing outward—to suit our very narrow tolerance of comfort and preference and pleasure.

Really, it is this capacity to alter and control our place, our world at all levels for efficiency, economy and predictability that epitomizes modern mankind's ultimate conquest and dominion over nature and his environment. Unlike our forefathers, we need accept none of the givens of where on the earth we live.

Nature is subject to our whims and malleable to the power of our technologies. What higher good is there than this, than to be free of the constraints of place?

How we think about place has undergone a sea change in two hundred years. Basic human biology and the fundamental workings of nature have not. We have allowed ourselves to be dulled to complacency by the prevailing political hubris that the health of humanity is measured more by an economic than a biological yardstick. This is a dangerous delusion to which we have succumbed.

I fear for our future if the current state of the physical world—our forests, parks, seashores, prairies, pastures and woodlots—continue over the next two hundred years to be reduced to nothing more than a quaint backdrop for SUV commercials or pleasant slips of scenery for our brief vacations away from the narrow comforts of our manmade cocoons.

No Place Like Home
Body and Soul Together

The Floyd County Harvest Festival and Homecoming celebration provided ample evidence, if any were needed, that we are proud of where we live.

Some come by that attachment to place by virtue of long family histories here, from ancestors who loved this land when the county was officially founded long ago. Others, like my wife and me, have come here more recently, traveling, living and working other places before settling down exactly and intentionally here. And now, it is Floyd we all recognize and celebrate as home—these particular back roads, communities, hills and valleys to which we feel a belonging and of which we are a part.

Those of us who shared in the Harvest Festival should not take this deep connectedness for granted. In the larger world and in recent decades, it has been freedom from roots that has been valued. This has given rise to a cavalier placelessness for those who lack allegiance or roots to any one locality or region.

"Back home" for many young rural Americans has become a place from which to escape as soon as possible, a heritage to replace with job, degree, and far-flung life plans that point them away from rather than back toward the soil from which they grew.

And so it was gratifying to talk to a young man on the ball field on Floyd's homecoming weekend and learn that he was making a considerable effort to swim against the current that is carrying his peers off to the big cities.

"Most of my friends in college who were from here have moved away to find work," he told me. "I didn't want to do that. I belong here, so I'm hoping to find a way to make a living and make this my home for good."

Though his college studies didn't prepare him to do so, this young man is literally turning waste into profit, and hopefully into a sustaining and land-friendly live-lihood so that his children can belong to the same places to which he belongs.

Appalachians by history have had a foot in two camps. We have a long past of rugged self-reliance and individualism grounded in the necessity of making do with what is at hand to craft a living or to merely survive. At the same time, those who came before us have nurtured a strong, almost sacred sense of belonging to the places we are from.

And these bonds of collective attachment run deeper and wider than just to the local hollers or hilltops of home. Our relationship with place is more communal than self-serving, shared, not private. On occasions like the recent county celebra-tion, the spirit of community and common care for the land is impossible to miss.

There is so much culture, history and talent in these southern mountains of which we can be proud; and in these times, those of us who call Floyd County home both accept and celebrate our uniqueness of relationship to this place.

Together, from our common values and love of this land, out of our diverse experiences and beginnings but with a common citizenship in southwest Virginia's present, people are talking and working together. It is our growing sense of belonging to place that is the common language that brings us closer. It is this land that informs our identity, and from which we take our energy and inspiration, and our hopes for the future.

But this wonderfully complex blend of culture and biology, geology and geography that we call home is a fragile treasure easily lost. Fortunately, we are spared the threat that our mountaintops will be removed for coal, as is happening to our west. But our waters can be depleted or despoiled. The landscape can be marred forever by solutions that leave behind aesthetic problems—or worse—for generations to come. And development and growth too fast or ill-suited to the land can bring difficult and persistent problems we will leave our children's children.

It may seem a romantic notion, this concept of "sense of place." But I believe there is something fundamental and crucial to Floyd's future that can come from a better understanding of it. We all feel its pull strongly, and though we are not able yet to find the words to explain everything that it means to us, we appreciate more than ever that there is no place like home.

Clutter: In the Eye of the Beholder
Within These Walls

Of course you are aware that January is "National Get Organized Month," right?

Logical in timing, this push toward a new cosmic orderliness comes in January when "to be better organized" is (or was for the few days it lasted) in almost all our top five New Year's Resolutions.

This is such a noble and necessary and universally-beneficial goal that perhaps the cause should be lifted up and made more prominent. Perhaps we should declare National G.O. Month as a 30-day-long ducks-in-a-row messiness moratorium during which we are all required to stay home to sort and file, re-box and re-pile, toss out and retool our lives into neat desktops, orderly closets, and alphabetically-labeled attic boxes and A to Z cooking spices all in row.

Let's see a show of hands out there in Readerville: how many think that the scourge of messiness and clutter should be fully and permanently banished from our kitchens and home offices, garages and attics, work places and the back seats of our cars?

Hmmm. Looks to me like there is a diversity of opinion on this matter, with maybe a preponderance of the ladies voting YES, and more of the guys voting NAH (or wisely abstaining from admitting in the presence of their She-E-Os a secret love of chaos in the Domestic Dumping Grounds).

The Professional Organizers (who prosper even as we wallow in our Hoarded Halls of Flotsam) are the mercenaries whom I believe to have birthed this par-ticular national month in much the same way that Russell Stover and Hallmark Cards have self-servingly poured gasoline on the tiny flames of several other trivial holidays. Let it be known, conspiracy-theorists, that revenues from the sales of the paraphernalia of organization have risen ten percent in the past five years. We're talking here about things like collapsible files, clear plastic boxes and bins, closet expanders, labeling devices, and drawer caddies. There are now thousands of full-time professionals who will consult with your organization (or disorganization as the case may be)—with your business, or clutter-impaired spouse or child—to get the mess off the desk, for good, forever, and for a small fee, of course.

But wait: there is a murmur among the milling messy masses of America who like themselves just the way they are. A mutiny is afoot. An anti-anti-clutter minority is rearing its unkempt head at last to make its collective voice heard above the tempered whimpers of the neatnics:

"Let us say YES to MESS!" cries the rabble, the untidy marginalized who now embrace their disorder disorder. Let us come out of our Fibber McGee closets and be proud of the (seeming) chaos that rules our lives. Let us stand unashamed of our pickup-sticks piles of books and flyers and shifting columns of pages ripped from three-year-old magazines. We resolve to stand tall amid our free-form, unbounded coupon collections, our random news articles from 1999 and the assorted clusters of bent paper clips that we might find a use for some day, year, or decade.

But let's call a truce for the moment between the White Gloves and the Pig Sty crowds, shall we?

The truth of the matter is that all of us, neat-nuts and order-disordered alike, suffer the modern burden of TOO MUCH STUFF. I think about this as I look around this house, built in about 1880, at which time there were only tiny closets under the two stairwells. The owners' one set of work clothes and one set of go-to-meeting and funeral clothes hung in a wardrobe in the bedroom and their unmentionables lived uncrowded in a small chest-of-drawers. The only paper in the house was the family Bible (and perhaps the Sears catalog for the outdoor reading room). Surely it was easier to be seen as neat when we weren't hauling arm loads of conspicuous consumerism daily across our thresholds, real and virtual.

But you and I live in an age afflicted with stuff, often accumulated as a measure of our worth and importance. We gather it around us as solace or diversion. We build walls of it to distance ourselves from the repugnant privations, from the sad impoverishments of the larger, less materially focused world. We readily get involved in an unmanageable number of hobbies and commitments and don't know how to say no—or what to do with the e-mails and junk magazines, warranties and instructions, bylaws or battery chargers that come with them all. Small wonder we can't seem to gain control of our piles.

The White Gloves want it all hidden (most especially if company is coming) to maintain the illusion of moderation and control. The Pig Sty folk say let it be. They know what's in each stratum of each leaning pile and suffer no illusions that there is not too much junk per square foot of surface. I gotta be me, they say, and I gotta have my stuff where I can reach it.

And so the Professional Organizers have their work cut out for them this month. And when they come down our road, they might as well just drive on by. One of us here on Goose Creek is hopeless and unrepentant. Just ask the lady wearing the white glove.

The Way We Were:
The High School Reunion
For the Time, Being

It was too long a trip from Floyd to Mobile for me to be comfortable with her going alone, though I dreaded the prospects of going with her. Everyone there would be a stranger. Maybe I shouldn't go at all. It was her home town where we would spend Thanksgiving weekend, her friends gathered there, her shared memories to be celebrated. I was just along to see that she reached safely that time and place beyond the realm of our long relationship, and got safely home again.

I knew it would be unsettling to be an outsider beyond the windows of her life, looking in on an era I did not spend with her, in a time when she was becoming who she would be when we met at Auburn our sophomore year and fell into something like love at twenty.

She spoke fondly and often of people who had once been her friends, found all across the country, now friends again, brought together by e-mail and conference calls. Their histories had become forever intertwined by the accidental thread of shared classrooms and stadium bleachers so long ago, and she would soon see them again after all these years.

It meant nothing to me except that it meant so much to her. I would go and support her as best I could. Besides, I had to admit—I was curious to see what it would be like to be with a hundred or more people who were my age, who had lived through my times. There would at least be that sixties connection between us, and maybe something from that to say to them.

It didn't make matters any easier that Ann was one a few who had initiated, organized and would be in charge of events over Friday and Saturday. For months, she had referred to the desktop computer's e-mail as her e-mail and I was banished to the laptop in the next room. For months, I went to sleep at the usual time while she stayed up clicking the keys furiously, helping coordinate the music that the DJ would play, making the name tags with pictures, planning the tour of the high school on Saturday afternoon.

For six months before the reunion, our present was immersed in her past, submerged in tiny black and white yearbook images of hairstyles from a lost time, symbols that spoke through rose-colored memory of simpler, more hopeful, mostly-happy days of youth growing up in the Deep South.

Friday's Meet and Greet under the vaulted atrium of the hotel lobby was an informal gathering. I consented to go down briefly to be introduced to a few of her most cherished friends. It wasn't long before I found myself standing alone among the anemic Ficus trees along the margins of the noisy crowd. I swirled the ice in my cup, conspicuously disengaged as slightly bent, gray-haired folk passed by for a quick look at my name tag. Was I another of their classmates grown unrecognizable over the decades?

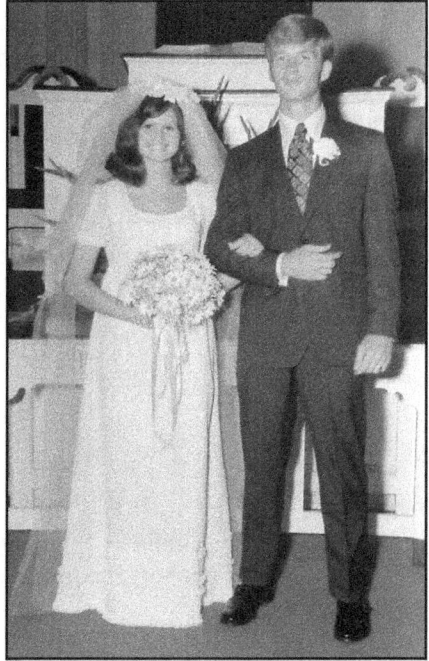

Cameras flashed. Hands were shaken and held. Hugs lingered, but the crowd milled about as if they had all just woken from a long, long sleep, only to find themselves surrounded by half-familiar faces.

When we've known someone for decades, somehow we never let go seeing them the way they were back then. And for her eyes, this crowd of late fifty-somethings were still the people of their pictures in the yearbook. Their high school faces and youthful, pre-adult personalities were that night who they had been to her then.

But I could not see through to the young people at their core. For me the encounter was unsettling—to be standing in the midst of so many iterations of just how old my body really is, even while the boy in me lived on, looking out through his eyes at these old strangers.

Soon, I slipped away to our room upstairs; she didn't even notice. I stood there in the dark quiet and watched the crowd—and my wife of thirty-six years, one of a hundred strangers mingling in the lobby, four floors below. Hugs, back slaps, handshakes, like so many ants touching antennae and moving on. We've come so far together to be so far apart for these two days, I thought. But such is the stuff of high school reunions, of separate realities that have made us who we are, for better or for worse.

And through all this, we've gone back in our conversations to roots apart in the pre-history of our relationship, and have had our own private reunion over Thanksgiving. We've found a common ground of understanding. In spite of the fact that we lived separate stories the first two decades of our lives and that this has made us see the world forever through different eyes, she and I can keep growing together, keep falling into something like love until we get it right.

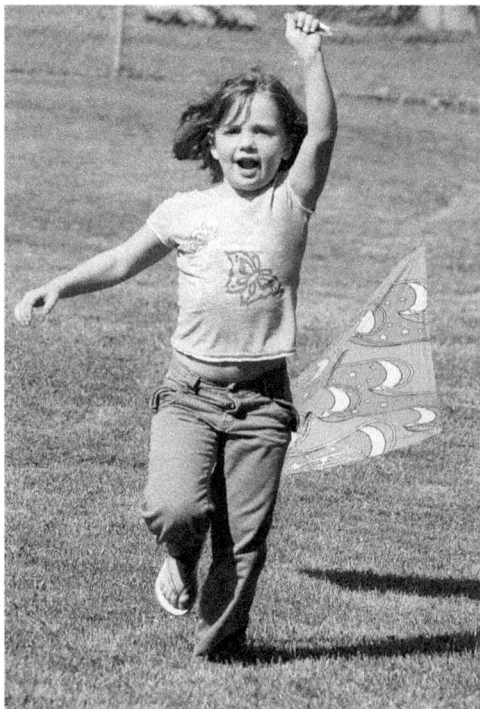

When Abby visits Granny and Dumpa on Goose Creek, they just give
her a bucket, a butterfly net, a big yellow dog, and an afternoon
outside. The rest of it, she makes up as she loses herself in play.

4

More than Child's Play: Getting Them Outdoors
Curious By Nature

A long, low building that had once been a sprawling grocery store was now a brightly-colored entertainment megaplex called "the Children's Fun Palace." The parking lot was filled with cars. None of us knew what to expect on this first visit, but it was obviously the place for kids to be on a warm, April day in the Midwestern town where my daughter lives.

Inside, the neon flashed and blinked. Bells and buzzers and sirens blared. Toddlers in diapers wailed and their older brothers and sisters whined for more quarters. I wanted to turn and run, but we had come for the purpose of entertaining our five year old grand daughter, Abby. And thank God, she would have none of it.

She became fretful and anxious after just a few minutes in the flood of noise and light, overwhelmed by the clash of careening video race cars and raygun-wielding aliens.

Our daughter Holli, Abby's mom, was apologetic. Other mothers had told her this was a good place to spend a few hot afternoon hours with kids. Holli knew that her parents, recently arrived from their quiet valley in Virginia, were stunned by the frenzy and glitz of the Fun Palace, and that they wanted something far different than this for their grand daughter's ideas about play. So we went to a park a half mile away, and the parking lot there was empty.

Within five minutes at the park, Abby had found the broken remnants of a tail-less kite. Her frolic with that free toy entertained us all under the blue spring sky for a wonderful hour that none of us will forget.

What a striking contrast we witnessed that afternoon between the old-fashioned play of children actively entertaining their bodies and imaginations outdoors and the modern, over-stimulating diversion that happens passively to kids almost exclusively inside and which may offer exercise for little more than the muscles of a thumb and one or two fingers.

"I like to play indoors better 'cause that's where all the electrical outlets are" explained one urban fifth grader I read about recently, a sign of our times. And I wondered: do we finally stand completely apart from nature? Have we lived past the days of free-range children at play?

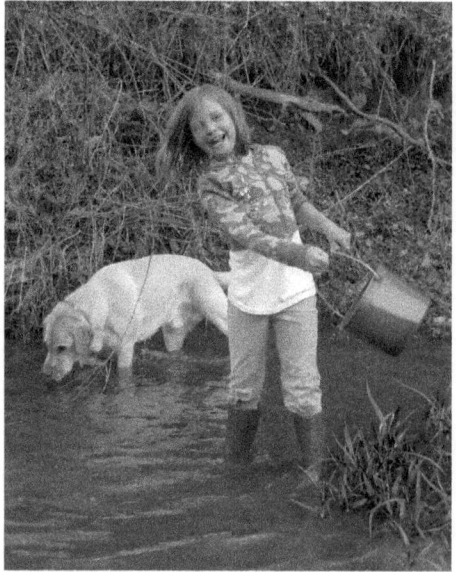

Ask just about anyone over fifty if being outdoors was important in their growing-up, and they'll tell of summer swimming holes and hide-and-seek in the woods. They will remember fondly and with perfect clarity winter skating on the pond behind the barn and building forts and catching crawdads in the creek. I couldn't imagine a childhood in which I had not entertained myself for hours in unstructured make-believe in the outdoors. When I was being punished, I was restricted to my room indoors, where these days, so many kids spend so much time by choice.

In his book, Last Child in the Woods, journalist and author, Richard Louv, calls this condition "nature deficit disorder." He describes the costs of our de-natured existence and also offers encouragement that we can do better than this for our children.

Louv makes the point that many of those who, in later life, harbor a deep appreciation for nature (some of whom go on to become conservationists or artists) often had moments of meaningful encounter with nature as children. But if our children are indifferent to the wonders, the beauty and serenity of nature, how can we expect their adult selves to care? If "the environment" for them now means only the ambient temperature at the shopping mall, why will they care in later life about the natural world's health and welfare?

The "Leave No Child Inside" campaign is just one possible path to give back to children the sounds, sensations and sensibilities that are lacking when they are not participants in the rhythms and cycles of the natural world.

But fortunately, in our small corner of the planet, the task of immersion in nature is not that hard. When Abby visits Granny and Dumpa on Goose Creek, they just give her a bucket, a butterfly net, a big yellow dog, and an afternoon outside. The rest of it, she makes up as she loses herself in play.

The Hairy Ones We Seldom See
Earth Companions

While the sighting of song birds and birds of prey are relatively common occurrences in season—though sadly much less so than once upon a time—seeing mammal species other than our dog has a low probability indeed as we walk our hills and woods near home.

There are fewer than a hundred mammal species in all of Virginia, and most of those are tiny and secretive. And so I was pleasantly surprised one day this winter week to see four different species of mammals in our valley, fellow creatures that share this land, this changing forest environment and climate, and perhaps a similar fate.

Though he usually spoils more potential animal observations than he produces for us, our dog's nose for prey and entertainment brought us two mammal sightings we would otherwise have missed this week.

To him, insectivores (moles and shrews underground) and small rodents (voles and mice in above ground nests of pasture grass) are lunch—little fur-wrapped tortillas and if not delicious, then at least no small excitement to catch and torment in cat-like fashion.

Yesterday, wonder-dog * Tsuga (a robust yellow lab) veered abruptly from beside us as we walked across the pasture, off in an instant at right angles to our path. He stopped suddenly, cocked his head, raised one front paw and pounced with two.

His front feet frantically churned the wet, sandy soil. (Had he smelled this subterranean creature from that distance, or heard it digging?) A half-dozen quick scratches later, and a dark grey velour sausage of an animal lay at our feet, eyeless, earless, and covered in dog spit.

Also that same walk, thanks to the dog's acute senses and agitated barking, we looked up to follow the flight of a flying squirrel that otherwise would have been perfectly happy to have remained hidden in the top of an old walnut as we passed underneath on our pasture road.

With the dog's loud alarm, the tiny squirrel opened his cape of fur (called a patagium, the same name this web-between-digits is given in bats) and launched himself from his perch to land midway up the trunk of a tree fifty feet away. Here's another small mammal rarely seen, though more abundant than you'd think. And if you ever do get close enough to examine these tiny squirrels, their large eyes will tell you they are creatures designed for the night.

We drive a bit less than two miles west when we leave home in Goose Creek Valley bound for Floyd, and rarely do we navigate this winding, climbing single lane road without spotting deer (which I refer to with little affection as "rats on stilts"), turkey, hawks or owls. But this week on a single pass, two other species appeared within a few hundred yards of each other.

About a mile up the road, I rounded one of the dozen treacherous blind curves— to which we have grown accustomed—to discover a distinctive creature I've seen a half dozen times before, digging in the wet margins of the creek at that same spot—a very large fox squirrel so light gray as to appear an albino.

His greatest risk of demise, other than his unusual and conspicuous hair color, is his fearlessness of passersby, who may not all be as interested as I am in merely admiring him there just beyond the edge of the road (though I hear fox squirrels make pretty tough eating).

Less than a minute's travel beyond the fox squirrel, a dark vertical shape moved quickly across the road and through the underbrush. Mostly black above and rust below, I took it at the first sighting to be a feral rooster.

Far from it: this was a red fox with a very dark tail, small as a house cat and feline-quick in its movements. Secretive as they are, we've seen not so many fox here, but find from time to time the remains of a songbird (juncos, mostly, judging from the feather mix) and now that our cat is gone, I credit these kills to fox.

Now I know none of these mammal sightings warrants calling in the camera crew from Wild Kingdom. But having these living beings around us and briefly close this week has given me a deeper sense of belonging here as one resident mammal among many.

We are not alone in these woods. Not yet. Life goes on below our feet, over our heads, at night while we sleep. I would like to think that this still relatively-diverse mammalian menagerie would grow in numbers because of how we treat the places we live—leaving the hollow trees we don't cull for firewood, the brush piles and weedy margins we let be, and by the pesticides we don't put on our soil—so our diversity can continue to consist of more than its interesting and varied mix of primates.

* Tsuga: "Soo-Gah". Genus name for Hemlocks, a family favorite, now in the process of disappearing from our forests forever. The dog was named in their honor, a botanical name that is fitting for his tree-hugging master in earthy Floyd County.

Plastic is Forever
Within Our Means

One word: plastic. Benjamin Braddock as The Graduate in the 1967 film may not have been at all interested in it. Meanwhile, America has swooned to the seduction of plastic after finding a generation ago that "cheap oil" could be made into so many versatile, colorful and inexpensive tools, toys and trinkets.

Every year, about 300 billion pounds of plastic are produced around the world. And the best thing about plastic that we discovered in the sixties is that it is practically indestructible.

And maybe the worst thing about plastic, Benjamin: it is practically indestructible.

Take plastic shopping bags, for instance. They are so prevalent across the landscape that I propose that they be named the new national flower. Lifted to bloom on tree limbs by the prevailing traffic-winds of speeding eighteen-wheelers, they are the most lofty blossom of humanity's love affair with plastic.

It's hard to believe it has only been some twenty five years since we were first faced with that awful but lightly dismissed environmental conundrum: paper or plastic? And overwhelmingly in recent years, the answer has been—you guessed it—plastic. Fully eighty percent of shoppers choose it. I read recently that "somewhere between 500 billion and a trillion plastic bags are consumed worldwide each year."

But wait. Let me set the record straight: that many bags are made and are utilized. But dear hearts, they are NOT consumed. They are NEVER really consumed. They are however, unfortunately, sometimes eaten—but more about that distinction in a minute.

So. Where do all those trillion plastic bags go when they disappear from our lives—the ones that don't end up in the high branches of roadside trees? First, let's watch a bag settle into Goose Creek right out my window here, blown from the back of someone's passing truck.

From the creek, it will wash in the next storm into the South Fork and on downstream, into the main flow of the Roanoke River. It may perhaps in high water become temporarily hung up in the branches of a piedmont stream-side alder. But eventually, it will find its way to the ocean. And there it will not be alone.

Let's follow our wayward bag to its not-quite-final end (a Styrofoam coffee cup or empty pop bottle would follow the same route) all the way into one of six ocean "gyres"—great swirls of listless ocean sometimes called the horse latitudes, where much of the world's floatable trash ends up in unimaginable abundance.

The North Pacific Subtropical Gyre between Hawaii and California can swell at times to twice the size of Texas and has come, just within our lifetimes, to contain many times more plastic than that area of ocean contains in living matter.

Bad enough that our trash plastic unaltered and whole can strangle an albatross or seal (six-pack holders are notorious for this kind of death) or choke a green sea turtle that fatally mistakes our ocean-drifting plastic bag for a tasty jelly fish.

But perhaps the most ominous thing about the durability of plastic is that it can, over long stretches of time, wear down by sheer mechanical action into smaller and smaller particles without reverting back to its constituent carbons and hydrogens.

Many millions of pounds of these tiny non-digestible particles are destined over decades, centuries perhaps, to float in the ocean currents. In time, almost microscopic bite-sized bits of plastic will be munched but not digested by zooplankton, the bottom tier of the marine food chain. These tiny animals by countless metric tons will be eaten by bigger and bigger fish, on up the food chain and into the grocery stores. And the plastic—and its constituents (a rogue's gallery of dangerous additives) lives on, and on, and on.

Consider this: "Except for the small amount that's been incinerated—and it's a very small amount—every bit of plastic ever made still exists." Each of us unthinkingly tosses into the environment about 185 pounds of plastic per year. And you have to wonder: do we need bottles that only briefly contain amazingly-expensive flavored water but persist empty for another 500 years?

Where does this leave you and me? Perhaps we are on the verge of a slow substitution of non-degradable with break-downable "plastic-like" shopping bags and six-pack holders and drink containers and Barbies and Kens that don't require fossil fuels. As nearby as Virginia Tech, new, less persistent polymers for this purpose are being created using chicken feathers!

So the next time the nice young man at the local market presents me with that impossible paper-or-plastic conundrum and I don't know how to answer, I'll have brought my used plastic bags from home for reuse or be toting a canvas shopping bag (it's a start, and something we can do in the near term). I'll smile as I imagine a green sea turtle off the coast of Myrtle Beach munching contentedly on a real, digestible, peanut-butter-and-jellyfish.

Thar's a Moose in Air Hoose!
Not Fish Nor Fowl

Adult language is embedded in the soft pink automatic machinery of the brain. Speech emerges reflexively, without thought or conscious plan—like breathing. Our tongues move with unconscious precision in the same way we take one step after another and find we've walked a mile without thinking about where our feet have been from one instant to the next. And yet we inevitably stumble in speech because no matter where we travel or live, we carry along with us the baggage of the language our ancestors left us. Be warned! This can carry you places you didn't intend to go. Here's the problem:

Down in that deep vault of language where vocabulary and syntax live also dwell the Rules by which our lips and tongue deliver the words we know: we call it Pronunciation. And once in place, it does not want to be disturbed. Ever.

While the Control Center of Language will allow in new words and let us weave them together with greater skill perhaps, it refuses to entirely relinquish to new habits the way we have spoken those words since we first heard them as children. You say tomato, and well…

As I child, I spoke Alabamian. And while I've been around the block a time or two since then and my dialect over time has morphed in many ways from the typical Dixie Drawl of my forebears, there are still a few words that I must consciously wrestle from the Department of Tongue Control if I want not to be misconstrued entirely or branded as a gump in my everyday conversation.

One of those words that crops up often in my speech is the little word our. I must be very careful here. If I let my deepest language reflexes take over, the word will come out Alabamian as ire—ire woods, ire creeks, ire children. And I will tell you a little story that explains my vigilance to avoid even such a slight slide of the terrible tongue—that tiny rudder that could steer your mighty ship into the Rocks of Absurd Misinterpretation.

Years ago and not long after we had moved to Virginia, we were having dinner with some new acquaintances, a couple from a county in far southwest Virginia. After dinner at a restaurant in town, the wife invited us to come home with them. She suggested "Why don't y'all just ride in air car?"

I honestly didn't know there was such a wonderful conveyance, but I prickled with anticipation at the possibility of traveling in such an advanced vehicle here in the hinterlands of Appalachia. (And I had been concerned before we moved to Virginia that this area might not be as technologically sophisticated as Alabama! Indeed! I was going to ride in an air car!)

You can imagine my disappointment when I discovered the trick that local dialect had played on me and before I learned to translate her air into my ire.

And a bit more in the way of cautionary tales from our How You Say It Department: A local Western North Carolina woman with whom I once worked left her small provincial world for a visit to New York City with coworkers. In a fancy restaurant, she placed her drink order, and when the waiter brought her a tall bottle in a sterling silver bucket of ice she said "the-us isn't what ah awdahd."

She had been very clear that she wanted "ahs tea" and so the waiter had obediently brought her Asti—an expensive sparkling wine—and not the sweet Carolina state beverage. Oops!

Pronunciation has recently become a matter of political correctness no less, so beware!

Department store Santas for a major chain in Australia have been instructed how to correctly express their season's greetings as they stand in their red and white costumes before the surging throng of expectant kiddies.

This year and from henceforth, they will exclaim "Ha Ha Ha!" with the idea that the former form familiar for generations might be mistaken as an endorsement of the world's purported oldest profession. I'm not making this up. And I have to wonder: would "He He He!" be banned as gender discrimination?

So during air holiday season just ahead, be careful little tongue what you say. And for all ire sakes, be careful how you say it!

Fred's Victory Garden
Body and Soul Together

As I contemplate the gardening year ahead, what comes to mind is the vintage Wide-World-of-Sports opening action that showed us the disparate fates of two ski-jumpers. Their success and failure will live forever in some of our chronologically-enhanced minds. Remember?

One successful skier is airborne, leaning forward, building speed down the ramp, then buoyant and balanced, graceful and solid in his landing; the other, ill-fated, off-kilter and out of control, he careens over the side of the jump, wind-milling arse over teakettle in the agony of defeat.

It could go either way every gardening year, I admit as I head out with my seeds, my hoe, and my hopes momentarily intact. Sadly, at the end of gardening year 2006, I was the second of those two jumpers—humiliated, humbled and broken. Sports fans gasped in horror. Ouch. That's gotta hurt.

I blamed myself, though I knew the garden's sad and sudden demise was surely due to matters beyond anything I could have done. Maybe it was the four inches of rain we had the week before the onset of Sudden Garden Death. Or, perhaps we were finally paying the chemical price for putting the garden in the only possible place it could go in our less-than-ideal rock-infested deep valley location: over the septic field. (Frankly, I thought I'd heard that grass—and veggies—were supposed to grow greener there!) I had the soil tested for excess chlorine, considering this possibility.

The total garden wipeout was all the more heart-breaking because at the end of the gardening year of 2005, we paid to have five walnuts cut from around the garden. We get little enough light in this deep holler, and the trees had grown tall and wide enough to cast a significant shadow. Also, you may know, their roots exude a toxin poisonous to competing plants—including those of the edible vegetable variety. (We bartered one large walnut trunk towards the oak desk under my keyboard now, and burned the tops for firewood, even though I think walnut makes more ash than heat.)

The other tragic fact about our 2006 garden's utter failure was that we had made its success a kind of sink-or-swim test of our self-sufficiency: let's work as if we are totally dependent on summer's produce alone for the coming winter's food. I set the bar high, and didn't even get airborne. We would have starved.

Okay. Here's the full confession part of this dreary tale: we have seen the enemy and it are us. Well, it are me. Yep, single-handedly I wiped out our garden from sheer ignorance in my gardening zeal. Soil tests in March '07 showed the soil was NOT ACID ENOUGH! Somebody (gulp) must have put too much alkaline wood ash (walnut mostly) and leaves on the soil. Mea culpa. The big OOPS. I have followed the advice given to bring our little plot back to a healthy pH, and we'll hope for the best.

The best. Now just what does that mean, in local gardening terms? Is the best we can hope for to create the lushest, tastiest and most tempting Deer and Insect Salad Park on Goose Creek?

As my daughter would say: you want some cheese with that whine?

I admit it: I'm discouraged. We have rectified my toxic attempts at organic soil amendment. We have removed the shade trees to maximize our sunlight, and repaired the five-strand electrified fence.

And yet, with all the hours of tilling, stooping, bending, pulling, hoeing, watering and coddling in the months to come, we may still suffer the agony of defeat. Make that "the agony of the feet"—deer feet—tramping the Swiss Chard, mincing the smooth spaces where I would plant fall greens, tramping down the waist-high corn. What's a gardener to do?

And I dream of the Fortress Garden. I see rat wire sunk two feet below the surface to keep out burrowing insectivores—moles and shrews—that would tunnel

their way into the stockade. Twelve foot posts are buried three feet into the earth, cemented in place, holding up a cattle-panel-reinforced nine-foot electrified fence. There is razor wire across the top. The entire structure is covered over by a drape of fine-mesh Kevlar netting to keep out the crows that would maliciously pull up the new bean sprouts, and then mosquito-netting on top of the whole thing, to hold out the cruel Japanese Beetles that turn vegetable leaves to lace, and the menacing eye-seeking ear-buzzing gnats of July that make a gardener slap his head silly.

But daydreams end, and life goes on, powdery mildew and blossom rot notwithstanding. And as I stand here on the leafless plain of our future garden in early May, I look around and imagine the greens and golds, reds and yellows of all the blessings that can come from the tiny seeds in my bucket, still embryo-like in their packets full of promise and hope.

You know, I bet that the guy that ended up in a crumpled heap off the edge of the ski jump eventually got back up and tried again. And so, too, will we. I'll get back to you in September with the judges' scores.

Two Hands Clapping
Within These Walls

I was commiserating with a writer I bumped into in the post office last week. To my self-pitful complaints that there was no wind in my writer's sails he came back with equal despair that, if he expected to ever get any writing done, he would have to find a far off desert island where he could hear his own thoughts.

I told him with some swagger that I wrote every day from a desert island and it was on Goose Creek in Floyd County. I half-believed at the time that this metaphor was true, but since then, I've had second thoughts.

Yes, I do feel at times the kind of serenity and isolation it takes to write from this sheltered place. We do live in secluded spot where outdoor sounds consist of the babble of creeks and wind on the ridges and only the occasional jet descending into Roanoke.

But inside, to be honest, this is rarely a desert island of writerly tranquility. In this room where I would join word to word rumbles a train station of clanging ideas, a raucous airport of criss-crossing trails in the sky of imagination, a corporation switchboard of neglected phone calls, and a stratified desk of white noise.

Bank statements half-reconciled shout in a shrill cry to be resolved; packages plead for mailers and addresses; ignored receipts multiply like rabbits. And hey, look at that browser page—what a great topic for a future blog post. I'll just make a few notes and…

The phone rings. The wife has just returned from town. And oh dread! I run the risk of losing hold of the thread I followed with such passion three minutes ago at the shore where desert island meets inner metropolis. I have to do better at organizing my domain.

✳ Clean off the desk of visible distractions. Let the phone ring and turn off the answering machine; if it's important they'll call back. (Yes, dear, I'm in the middle of making a list...)

✳ Set a timer and only get up to stretch. Return to center. Prohibit mental intruders. Reward yourself if you succeed.

✳ Keep a clear focus on the prize; know what it is, what it will take to get there, steel yourself. (Yes, I'm coming. Be just a minute...)

✳ Find and stick with a consistent organization method that keeps me from having to reproduce steps. Ask for help when others can do something more efficiently and expertly than I can. (No I'm not ignoring you. I'll bring in the groceries in a bit. I'm just concentrating...)

✳ Keep a checklist of tasks completed to let me see I have made progress. Take out the screens and clean the windows in my junky room that I should be ashamed of.

✳ Vacuum the rugs, bathroom and kitchen floors (can't I see the dog-hair tumbleweeds? Am I blind or just a slob?)

✳ Throw out those empty boxes from the new addition, a room that started out being the ANNex but has recently morphed, she says, into the FREDex.

✳ Sweep the front walk and dust off the porch furniture before company comes this afternoon for dinner to see that some of us live like pigs.

Oh never mind. I seem to have lost my initial focus. How is that possible here on this tranquil desert island? I suppose I should have confessed to my writer buddy in the post office that I am not the only person marooned here, and to my horror, instead of palm trees, the beaches of Solitude Shores here are infested thick as Kudzu with the aggressively-invasive Honey-do Vine.

A Dad Remembered
For the Time, Being

So here we are, empty-nesters, sandwiched once more on the late spring calendar between Special Sundays for mothers and fathers. Our adult offspring (the term we substitute in recent years for the word "children" when describing our matured brood of two) live far away and it's easy to misplace even the memory of the satisfaction and anguish of having actively, presently, physically been someone's parent so long ago and far away.

But here let me confess that I have a curmudgeonly and cynical opinion of these parent-spousal "holidays" as being manufactured for the bottom line of the greeting card and box candy companies.

I will also admit that at times, to be remembered in the small way of a special phone call, a hand-written letter or a cross-country trip on these designated days of appreciation are, well, genuinely appreciated.

Saved, Remembered, Found: a father's day poem—a toast (and cleverly veiled roast) for Father's Day, received from our son, Nathan, then a single scholar just moved to British Columbia, and today married and moving into their first owned home in Missouri—still far too far away.

I thought I would share Nate's poem with you this Father's Day in the hopes that it might help you to recall: that seeming crisis in your relationship with your dad that looking back was so silly you can laugh about it now; the way you respected him but never got around to telling him because at the time, he rightfully thwarted your idiot dreams; the lessons he taught you by example, good and bad; and the pride you know he has when he hears from you, a grown or growing young man or woman who occasionally takes the time to say "thanks, dad."

Do consider using this "poem" as a model, and give a single page an hour of your time, a gift to give your dad this year, while there's time. Chances are, he'll never forget it.

A Father's Day Poem For Dad, 2004

For all the times you made me hold that darned ladder.
For all the times you said, "if you throw that tennis racquet again, we're going home,"
and I threw the tennis racquet again, and we went home.
For that time you wanted to go hiking in the Smokies, and I wanted to go to Amy Harris's
pool party, and I pitched such a fit halfway to the Smokies so you turned the car around
and drove us home at breakneck speeds, only to give in half an hour later after I pitched
another fit, and we went to the Smokies, and had a nice time.
For beating me every time at every sport and every game, many years after I was sure
I was better than you.
For the thirty-seven times you told me the name of the same green-metallic beetle, while
each time I was thinking about some girl or some song I'd like to write, or some song I'd
like to write about some girl, only half an hour later to see a green metallic beetle, and
wonder what kind it was.
For the times you crushed between your fingers something sweet-smelling, or sharp-smelling,
or minty-smelling, or putrid, and shoved it toward my nose, saying, "Nature snort!"
For all the arguments we've had about religion, and all the agreements we've had about politics.
For all the times we've called each other "smart-a—," audibly or otherwise.
For every time you should've made fun of me for the way I split wood,
and the vast majority of times that you did.
For all those really stupid ideas I've had, which you vehemently opposed,
until you knew I'd go through with them anyway, at which point you supported me.
For all those trips I've taken, and you've secretly worried about, even while you tried to
project all your concerns for me onto "my mother."
For teaching me to light the water heater—and to rake with full, efficient strokes, and
curse at the weed-whacker, and spread the peanut-butter clean out to the crust.
For all the creative ways you punished me, with just enough consequence to sting,
and just enough humor to tell stories about later.
For finding your craft, your voice, and a fulfilling sense of place—for living my aspiration
and giving me a sense of belonging, even as odd as I feel to live vicariously through my father.
For all those times, all those lessons, all your friendship and love, this father's day
I bought you an ice-cold bottle of beer,
Which I'm drinking now as I write you this poem,
All the while thinking, man, he would've enjoyed this.
Thanks, Dad. Love you. I'll spot you that beer sometime. — NLF

The HolliBear Family Tree
For the Time, Being

Our daughter's name is spelled Holli, but it is after the prickly plant with the bright red berries that she is named. And so, growing up, she was sometimes Holli-berry, later shortened to Holli-bear, and even now, her husband calls her simply "bear." She has two cubs of her own, this poem written just before the first of them was born—Abby now eight, and as this poem predicts, very like her mother.

I think that there could never be
A thing more peculiar than a Family Tree
Whose roots some trace back to Adam's impediment,
Or others, to slime of Precambrian Sediment

My own branches flow through the young Holli tree
And more fruits like herself now soon there will be
That genes might effect this, we hardly can doubt'em
And my sprouts mutated with quirks all about'em

Her mother and I weren't
prepared for the job
Our First Family nursery was
somewhat macabre
We pruned and we grafted, it
took so much care
But we managed, at our
best, to harvest a Bear

She growled and she scowled
if the soup didn't suit,
And now she herself will
be tasting that fruit
She'll weed and she'll water
and shovel manure
But her little fruitlets just wont listen to'er

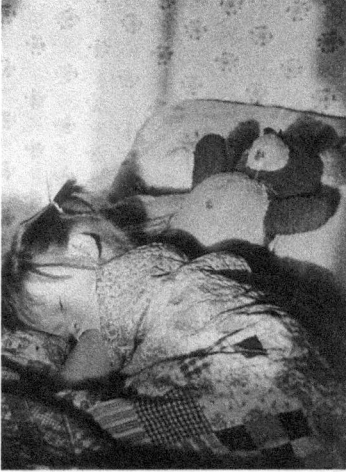

They'll send out their tendrils and grow toward the light
In their way, when they please, they won't be polite
Til one day like magic in horror they'll see
The fruit doesn't fall very far from the tree

And so in our times now of former twig-bending
We look up ahead to see our garden ending
But others we've nurtured and their gardening spouses
Anticipate tending their own strange greenhouses.

Then we who reside down a notch on the arbor
Give our tools a rest in parental safe harbor
When our kids come visit with several bambini
We'll politely decline, we don't need more zucchini!

And many years later, they'll inquire of beginnings
And wonder of their roots and gene-underpinnings
She'll tell them the cause of their rural aberrance:
Their American Gothic maternal grandparents!

Floydians waiting for fireworks...simply enjoy being with one another doing not much at all under a warm summer sky. Sometimes, less is more.

5

Abby and the Queen Anne's Lace
Curious By Nature

You might know Queen Anne's Lace. Its flat-topped inflorescence graces many meadows and roadside margins across a good swath of the country.

What you may not have noticed (but probably will, now that you know) is that there is often a single purple-black flower in the center of the cluster. Why? Even the experts can't say for sure.

Once when Abby was visiting, I challenged her to explore the pasture margins to find me a Queen Anne with a dark central flower. It didn't take long for her to locate one by herself. She got really good at finding them, and it became a kind of game for us. "I bet those over there has it" I'd challenge, and off she'd run to see if I was right or wrong.

"Look Dumpa!" and she motioned me over to have a look at her discovery. There in the center of the flat-topped disk of tiny white flowers was a strikingly brilliant Deptford Pink she'd found among the tall grasses. She'd secretly slipped it into the center of the Queen Anne's Lace.

She grinned from ear to ear, telling a visual joke she knew grandpa would get. But more than the humor, I had the deep soul satisfaction of knowing I had taught our own personal next generation something worth remembering about the natural world.

She showed me in this AHA! discovery that she had learned to be surprised by nature (such a valuable expectation in the outdoors) and that she could use those new facts to surprise and delight others—a marriage of knowledge and humor, of precious and precocious wisdom. Yes!

September's Tiny Zoo
Earth Companions

I have confessed to you before my (and my hapless wife's) checkered association with snakes and so I suppose it's a short step to admit that I also have an inordinate admiration as well for insects—for joint-legged animals (arthropods) in general, I suppose, even including spiders. There. I've said it. They have fascinated me for countless hours over the course of a long life as a bug-watcher. Here's why.

In miniature inside an armor-plated exoskeleton of a crayfish or millipede, wasp or butterfly exists the same working units—muscles, nerves, vessels, cells, tissues and organs—that sustain a human or an elephant or a brontosaurus on a larger scale of space and time. Here on the planet long before us, the insects have become specialists with marvelously unique job descriptions or "niches" in their inherited life settings of desert sand or ocean floor, under tree bark or pasture soil. Let me just describe a few of those we find along Goose Creek in September.

A thoughtful neighbor brought me a gigantic immature insect in a bucket last week. Oh Joy! It had been years since I'd seen a Hickory Horned Devil—a hideously beautiful caterpillar that might just as well have come direct from the lot of a B-grade science fiction movie as from a modern-day forest floor. This blue-green sausage-sized monster is the unlikely preparatory stage required to build the elegant Regal Moth, a beast and beauty story if ever there was one.

You'd hardly think something lovely could come from the intentional ugliness designed into this largest of North American caterpillars with its orange, re-curved and thorny "antlers" (which actually are harmless to touch).

Today's beleaguered forests are not the same as the undisturbed forests to which these creatures have adapted over their long history. This species—an obligate forest dweller—is one of many insects in decline across the country. So if you find one, show it to the neighbors—like mine did!

As fall approaches and summer vegetation begins to droop and brown, milkweed and goldenrod are both likely to harbor colorful and interesting species.

Common milkweed has been a plant-distribution success story as fields and pastures were cleared from the original virgin forest of the continent. Air-borne seed on silky parachutes spread across America, and with the milkweed as a food source, the Monarch butterfly and other insect species also spread.

The remnants of our wild milkweed look pretty rough by this time of year, dog-eared, raggedy and full of milk-weeping holes. The grasshoppers use it as resting spots, and inch-long Assassin Bugs lie in wait for them behind a leaf. When dinner comes, they spear it, and suck up its juices with their needle-like mouthparts that also contain an inner straw for this purpose. Also called the "Wheel Bug" for the toothed curve on its back, this is one to watch but not touch, as its bite can be painful.

Here I should mention that this bestiary of creatures on the milkweed is likely to have hard times ahead. While it's important to insects like the Monarch butterfly, milkweed is just that—a weed—to those who grow crops or cattle on their land. This plant is being exterminated across large parts of its former range. So if you have milkweed growing around the perimeters of your place, please leave it—or even plant an intentional "butterfly garden" of milkweed and other host plants with the idea that species other than man and his animals need to make a living, too.

Lastly, check out the goldenrod, wonderfully crawling with a little community of specialist insects who come there for mating or dinner. One to look out for is the Locust Borer, an elongate beetle that you'll hesitate getting too close to at first. With its yellow and black stripes it looks for all the world (and this is no accident) like a yellow jacket. (Notice a distinctive black "W" across the tops of the outer wings.)

This is a great example of "protective resemblance" in which a harmless animal wears the garb of a noxious one. Just don't do like I did this week in my haste to show Ann this sign of fall: I quickly scooped up a Locust Borer from a goldenrod to show her, and when I opened my hands, I'd also captured a little bumblebee hiding on the back side of the flower cluster!

They'll be gone soon, the insects of autumn, as much a part of the march of seasons as the passing of the wildflowers or migration of the songbirds. So do pay attention to the little zoo of fall invertebrates just out your back door, in your meadows and woods. They offer all sorts of lessons for those who take the time to look carefully at the small things close at hand.

Whose Rights, Whose Ways?
Within Our Means

Under a clear, blue, late November sky I stood boot-ankle deep in the cold water of Goose Creek, thankful for the respite from a spate of bitter, blustery days the week before, thankful, too, for this windfall firewood that straddled the creek near home. Its bare-pronged roots had washed clean since the little oak slumped down the rocky face of the bluff.

An opalescent sheen shimmered past with the slow flow of the creek as I cut into the thin, straight trunk. I quickly realized to my horror that I had just created this slick with the bar oil from my saw. On dry land I would never have noticed this environmental cost of doing business, but here on the water was the visible effluence of my work, a buoyant rainbow rippling downstream.

My thoughts returned just then to the meeting only a few days earlier where I heard American Electric Power (AEP) officials claim that petroleum products (including bar oil) from mechanical clearing of their right-of-ways would leave behind more dangerous chemical residues than did their spraying. A specific herbicide incident this summer had been the source of community concern culminating in a citizens' meeting in Cave Springs.

And with more than 46,000 miles of distribution lines and the cumulative hundreds of square miles of clearing in them in the eleven-state region serviced by AEP alone, it was not just Crystal Creek at issue in that Roanoke gathering. In my rubber boots standing in the creek, it dawned on me that this is an issue of national reach and relevance.

Power lines must traverse hundreds of miles, taking the shortest distance between power plants and destinations of use at businesses or homes. Those cleared corridors will necessarily bisect city, farm and forest. The energized wires are dangerous and must be held well out of harm's way. The lines, too, are prone to sway and sag and tree damage, and their access for repair must be maintained.

Meanwhile you and I will raise all kinds of heck if our service is interrupted, our trees are cut or our water quality or our health is placed potentially at risk. Can we have our cake and eat it too?

Those power lines and their clearings are only there because we are here. The denuded and unnaturally straight-edged gouges that cut across the contours of our mountains are not pretty but regrettably, they are necessary in our time of history, given consumer electricity addiction and utility mandates to feed those habits.

Our bright rooms at the flip of a switch come at a price. Like coal, utility right-of-ways are a cost of doing the electricity business that require a total of some two billion dollars every year just to maintain. However, this is a human enterprise in transition.

I can imagine a day hopefully not too many decades ahead when the coal under Appalachian mountaintops will stay where it is and each home or business will generate its own electricity with technologies we can only now imagine. Until then, with rights-of-way issues we are going to have a problem in need of solutions short of a total fix. These will not be problems solved satisfactorily by using a bigger chemical or mechanical hammer or by more vociferous protests.

More people within and outside of the electrical industry are coming to appreciate that working with rather than against nature on this issue is the wisest course. Managing corridors to create understory vegetation suited by its growth habit to be both attractive and productive while posing no risk to the power lines overhead is part of the "right tree in the right place" program gaining increased attention.

Right-of-ways course through wetland, meadow, cove forest and coniferous woods—whatever lies in their path—creating edge effects and early successional stages in every conceivable kind of plant and animal community. Botanists, ecologists, hydrologists, wildlife biologists and teachers of every stripe are concerned and involved in helping utilities like AEP become better stewards of these imminent domains that belong to all of us.

The next linear utility clearing you see on your travels through your local landscape represents a single thread of the larger tapestry of our dependence on electricity produced for us and carried to us at no small environmental cost. We should not take the work our utilities do on our behalf for granted, nor they our collective dedication and concern for the common wealth we share together.

Digital Reading: More Taste, Less Filling
Not Fish Nor Fowl

I am not the focused, careful reader I remember myself once to have been, and at least in part, I blame the keyboard under my hands and screen in front of my face. All of my writing and far too much of my reading in the past several years has moved from paper to computer. In this transition, my time-worn and once-essential methods to take in, store and digest information have been replaced.

I have morphed from a cud-chewing slow-digesting reader of entire magazines or books into an information butterfly flitting about to sip snips from one open program, one web site, one desktop data-mine to another.

This trend toward broad but superficial hyperlinked sampling rather than deeper forms of reading concerns me even as I'm continually amazed at how marvelously accessible information has become to the average Internet user. We really should be growing smarter as a species, but there's scant evidence I can see that this is yet the case.

I was already wallowing in this personal angst when I spotted an online Atlantic Magazine story called *"Is Google Making Us Stupid?"* by Nicolas Carr. I bookmarked it in my browser, saved some clips from it, and then as is so often the case for the browsing window shopper I've become, I flitted off to skim and snip something else. Only after buying the July/August copy of that magazine off the rack at the Roanoke airport terminal and reading Carr's article all the way through—holding it in my hands turning pages on the plane—did the impact of its (too long for web-reading) 4000 words sink in.

The author concludes that, yes, we are in the midst of significant change in the ways we read and research documents, and in the ways we think and remember things. With regard to the latter for instance, why bother remembering how to spell, do math, remember a poem or recall your grandmother's telephone number or even your own? We now have silicon memory of one kind or another at our fingertips—our text-and-image based outboard brains that do the heavy lifting of remembering, spelling, adding and mapping our way home.

More and more, we read horizontally, gathering staccato chunks to quickly glean the main point of an article online where once we would have had to invest the time and energy to read it deeply at the library downtown and jot longhand notes. Now, we can come back to it any time we like to finish reading it all. But do we?

Reading on the web has put efficiency and immediacy above comprehension or synthesis, and this may be weakening our ability to make persistent, deep mental connections in what we read. Reading, after all, is not "etched into our genes the way that speech is" Carr reminds us. Reading is a skill set new to our species since the advent of the written parchment, the printed page, then the typewriter and finally the computer keyboard that has so drastically added to the volume and availability of words-in-print (that are mostly never printed in the old-fashioned sense).

We are at risk of becoming "pancake people—spread wide and thin," filled with content but lacking the deeper understanding of our place in the world and its literature, culture and history. We connect to everything, comprehending little of it. But certainly there is still an important place for the fuzzier associations that come from a deeper if slower and less "productive" kind of page-reading and pondering once done offline at libraries and churches, family dens and park benches.

Will we have to pull the plug on Google and Wikipedia, prohibit cut and paste, avoid hyperlinks or digital bookmarks to save our morphing brain's ability to read, think and reason?

I can only say that, for me, it would probably be wise to balance today's digital efficiency against the doing of things the slow, low-tech, unplugged old fashioned way: to spend an hour on the front porch with a good friend or a good book; to take unhurried walks in the woods and slow drives down Floyd County back roads with no radio, cell phone or GPS beeping; and in quiet places to be content to offer to the mind questions and perplexities whose answers matter and do not require drop down menus or dialogue boxes.

To put too fine a point on it, I might consider a question about priorities asked long ago: What good does it profit a man if he gains the whole world and loses his soul?

Our Greatest Resource: Each Other
Local Color

A man, his wife and young daughter stopped by my table at the Fourth of July fireworks event. He had heard a recent interview on WVTF and he wanted to talk with me about it—but not so much my book as about the fact from the interview that I have been searching for a new direction for my life now that our children are grown and we have settled permanently in Floyd County.

It did not take long to learn that this man was searching, too: for involvement, for connections and for community. Turns out, he and I were asking some of the same questions about life's purpose near or after retirement, questions about finding oneself in and contributing to a new community, and about the future growth and change in the county. And so our conversation lasted more than an hour that late afternoon as storm clouds gathered and the sky darkened over the high school ball field.

"Will you look at that!" he said, as we surveyed the green lawn before us, strewn with young and old, standing, sitting and lying on blankets in little clumps and clusters. "This is what it's all about. What a simple, peaceful scene. There's not a thing flashy or pretentious here, nothing fancy or high-tech or loud—just people enjoying one another's company."

His comment shifted my thinking and our conversation in the direction of a report I'd read recently. A sad situation exists in America, the very opposite of what we were seeing before us on the ball field at sunset. According to this study, Americans are more socially isolated than they were in 1985 when the average respondent to the survey said they had three close friends.

Sadly, in the new study, nearly a quarter said they had "zero" close friends and more than half said they had "two or fewer". Someone has said that "people watch Friends on TV. They don't have them anymore." Intimacy within families is down, too.

The reasons for this increasing isolation are not hard to find—in today's larger numbers of divorced or single adults; in longer commutes, longer and more stressful workdays. Also to blame are the larger percentage of people living in cities and suburbs, the loss of sidewalks and front porches, and the trend toward cocooning. Families rarely sit to meals together, and the most well off are isolated in their private spaces around computers, televisions, music and movies inside their fortress McMansions.

We live in an era of declining "social capital"—a term used and fully elaborated in the book, *Bowling Alone*, published in 2000 by Robert Putnum. This author and others suggest that social capital is a key component to building and maintaining democracy.

Americans are far less connected to each other than we once were, on average, and this bodes poorly for our cohesiveness as a culture. Interestingly, even our physical health seems to be connected to being connected. Our chances of dying are cut by a quarter simply by joining and regularly participating in one club or organization, and in half by joining two.

And as I stood there chatting with my new acquaintance, I wondered aloud: might Floyd and similar smaller, off-the-beaten-path places in rural America persist as tiny islands of relative social well-being? Is it possible in places such as this to resist or at least slow the erosion of connection between neighbors and

kin, to avoid the atrophy of personal accountability and care that is so common now in many of the burbs?

Because of the overall pace and scale of things in Floyd and like places, maybe those who live in them are more willing to reach out and participate, to acknowledge the need for one another, to help a neighbor. And maybe here, more than in larger, faster places, there is a growing awareness of the value in "local"—for our foods, our fun, and our friends. But then, maybe this is only a rural fantasy, wishful thinking that we could somehow swim against the growing tide of alienation from social belonging.

But for me, looking out over the field of Floydians waiting for fireworks that balmy night was comforting evidence that many still value slowness in sit-down meals and laid-back waiting-for-dark social events on the lawn, a commons where we simply enjoy being with one another doing not much at all under a warm summer sky. Sometimes, less is more.

Wood Heat: Hearth And Home
Body and Soul Together

Our move from Alabama to Virginia in 1975 introduced us to real winter, and our southern bones were not at all prepared. That first season of snow and ice, to stay warm, my young family had to eat our morning cereal sitting on the cast iron radiators. We knew early on that there must be a better way to keep from freezing indoors. We bought our first wood stove for reasons of sheer survival.

The day they delivered our Fisher Momma Bear stove, I thought we'd conquered winter's cold at last. But to feed our cast-iron heater, we owned neither truck nor chain saw. With Ann on push and me on pull, we bow-sawed our wood from deadfall by permit from the National Forest. We hauled it home in a Datsun hatchback, full down on its rear shocks, and split it piece by gnarly piece with an axe. This was the famous wood you've heard about that heats you twice (or more). For a naïve immigrant, the energy that goes into wood heat was a shocking lesson in simple living. Other lessons learned by the novice country mice that year included creosote. And flu fires. But those are stories for another time.

As we grew into our new southwest Virginia lifestyle and became comfortable with the rhythms of the heating year, I began to appreciate that 'hearth and home' are words that do truly belong together. When the cold winds whistled over the roof and the windows glazed with ice, family life was centered around that black box with the kettle hissing on top. The kids sprawled on the floor beside it and played dominoes. Ann sat in the high-backed chair with cross-stitch in her lap while I read or played the guitar in the warmth of wood we'd gathered from our own hillsides.

Thirty years and a hundred cords of hardwood later, I still enjoy the heat of wood, but I'm not quite as energetic now about the gathering of it, or the splitting, or stacking, or toting as I once was. The ground, it seems, gets a bit farther away from my hands with every passing year, and I swear a cord of wood didn't used to be so dog-gone heavy. But we'll hold out against the temptation of alternatives, especially now that other forms of heat are so expensive and might not be consistently reliable through life's storms to come.

The trees will continue to die and fall in our little valley, and it seems wasteful to give away such a windfall of energy to the decomposers on the forest floor. I'll be obliged by habit and my frugal nature to bring in the wood for yet another winter to feed this insatiable iron pet that lives with us. But there are other reasons to burn wood. I know this will sound strange, but the wood stove does seem like a family member, and it wouldn't be Virginia winter without it in our home.

The wood stove's care and feeding for the next six months will be as essential as our own eating and breathing. We will open its mouth and feed it often; we will check its temperature to make sure it becomes neither too hot nor too cold and we'll watch its breath out the chimney for signs of congestion. After feedings we will clean up the crumbs with a small brush and a dustpan. All winter long, we will pay homage with split oak, locust and ash—offerings to this insatiable, revered, cast iron symbiotic creature in our midst.

From these first brisk, gray fall days until the crocus and bloodroot pop up in the sunshine of April, the stove will be the first thing we care for each morning, the last duty we attend to every winter night. Before bedtime, we will sit in our chairs and watch the flames leap behind the glass door of the stove, and nod in the drowsy glow. From our bed in the dark, we'll hear it purring contentedly in ticks and pops as it warms, and we will fall asleep in its flickering light.

Things That Go Beep in the Night
Within These Walls

Let me tell you at the very beginning of this story that our dog is generally a well-adjusted, self-assured, yellow lab of normal intelligence and disposition.

This is not to say that, like all of us, he doesn't have his own eccentricities. I must report, for instance, that he is obsessive about butterflies. We can't tell if he loves them or hates them, but for certain, he is far more interested in catching their shadows that race across our yard than in the actual insect.

Convinced that these dark moving shapes disappear underground, he follows them at great speed across the gravel road or edge of the pasture to catch them before they go subterranean. With the warmer weather, our yard will become pock-marked with his attempts to dig up those burrowing butterfly shadows from down there with the moles.

Also some might consider it a bit unusual for an animal with such well-developed incisors that his favorite treat is a big wedge from a head of cabbage. Still, considering the eclectic local food preferences in our county, this mixed diet of cole slaw and butterfly shadows might not be all that odd.

And this particular dog's political leanings are most definitely toward the pacifist end of the spectrum, again not all that odd hereabouts. Given the least edge on our conversations (even if only animated and not agitated) the dog places his body between us as arbitrator, appeasing first Ann, then me, then back again. He is a conflict-averse, peace-loving, vegan flower-child of a

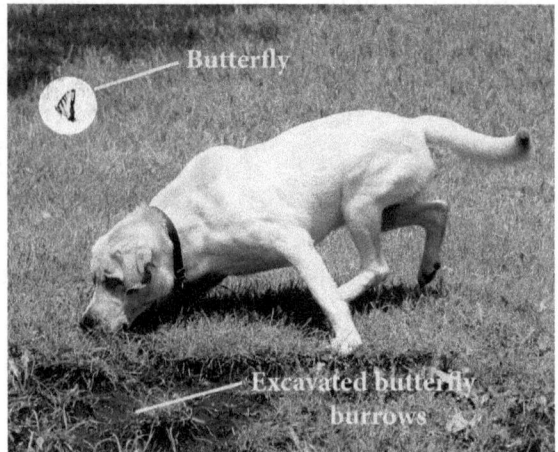

Butterfly

Excavated butterfly burrows

dog. So we smile awkwardly and speak in forced soft tones, even at those times when we are as temperamentally compatible as Keith Olbermann with Ann Coulter—for the dog's sake, you understand.

But as I say, even considering all these bits of oddness, Tsuga generally has run on a pretty even keel around here. Until yesterday.

"What in the world has gotten into the dog?" Ann wondered.

He bounced up and down at the back door, so frantic to get outside I thought he might jump through the window glass if he could. Is it another dog, you suppose? Well, if he'd heard another dog, then we certainly didn't want to let him out. We tried to distract him with a chunk of banana in his Kong, but he would not be consoled or diverted.

Agitated and filled with doggy dread of an invisible demon, he slithered around the edges of the kitchen, following Ann into the laundry room. Pressed into the angle between the washing machine and dryer, he hid his face in her robe.

"Maybe he's sick and needs to do something outside we wouldn't be happy for him to do inside" I suggested, and we hoped he wouldn't bolt off down the road as we opened the back door for him to escape.

He trotted straight to the far side of the drive over against the bank and just sat there, looking back toward the house, trembling.

After five minutes, he hadn't budged. Well then. It wasn't to puke or poop he wanted out so badly. I called him in. He refused. I threatened. He refused. How very odd. I gave up and left him peering fretfully at the back door as I closed it and headed back to whatever it was I had been doing at the computer before this episode of canine neurosis.

From the front room came a vaguely familiar sound, off and on intermittently, out of the computer speakers—an instant message notification—something that happens very infrequently around here. But then, it had only been about a week ago that I received a GoogleTalk invitation, and when the little BaBink! notification sound went off, the dog...

That's it! A simple computer sound pushed the dog's freak-out button. Go figure. I wonder where's the threat in this? Is there a frequency we can't hear that hurts his ears? Or is it fear that makes him tremble and cower—a terror that overcomes him, as if this were the scream of a Jurassic beast lurking somewhere in his species-memory?

But maybe, after all, this is simply one of those inexplicably irritating sounds we can't quite explain that rubs us the wrong way. Tsuga cringes at this computer alarm, but the dog would have no negative reaction at all from the sound of fingernails scraping down a dry chalkboard. Or Musak.

Shudder. I just had the terrible waking day dream that the dog here was offered a chance to write this story. I could see it clearly—a very long exposé—page after page of oddball things only a family dog could know about his quirky humans and ought never, ever to tell.

Ann says in Heaven, the dogs hold the leash and the treats. And Tsuga swears he's taking notes, and he's not going to forget.

For Better or For Worse: The Wedding
For the Time, Being

Ann and I will be leaving soon for St. Louis for our son Nathan's wedding. He is our only son, our youngest child, so our nest becomes truly empty now. When we return to Floyd on Monday, will the world look quite the same?

On the scale of human happenings, a wedding is a small thing. They happen every day to other people's children. The silly throwing of rice and confetti outside a church is different, though, when it falls on your child's shoulders and you send them off to start a new family. No matter how much we want to want to let them go, parents cling to the parts played in the long stories of our children's lives for so many years, and it takes some time to accept the new arrangements.

Nate will marry not just a woman but a family, and the part he plays in our own story for a while will seem distant and diminished. But we found a plastic bin of photographs this week while we were hunting for the Christmas wrapping paper and this has brought us some reassuring portraits of our family chronicle, past and future.

When those worn pictures of the times of our lives are spread out before us on the kitchen table, we see that we've let them go before, so often, so painfully and fearfully. Our children are never exactly the same on the other side of these passages; but then, we wouldn't want them to be unchanged by graduations and weddings, travel hellos and goodbyes.

Look. Here is a picture of our daughter who was married in 1997—the summer I moved to Floyd and lived on Walnut Knob that lonely year before Ann could move up to join me. Talk about your empty-nestings. That wedding, I suppose, was hardest on me, the father of the bride. And here is the picture someone took of the bride's customary dance with her father; fortunately, he's facing away from the camera so that you can only see her happy tears to the tune of Butterfly Kisses. At least I won't be expected to dance with the groom in the wedding in St. Louis.

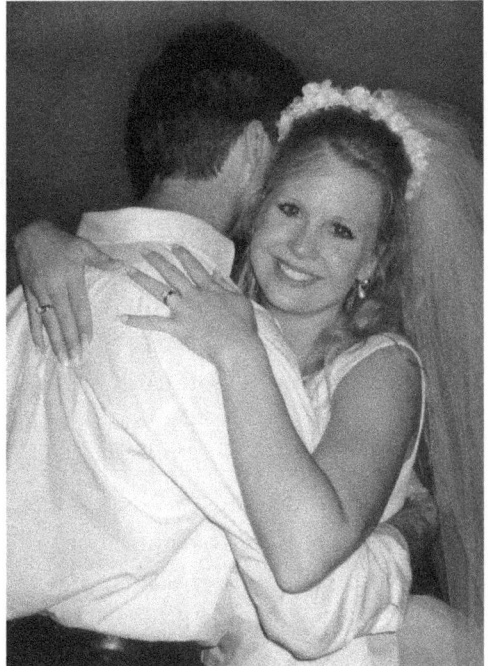

I'm not sure, but I'm hoping that the father of the groom is not required to participate officially in a son's wedding. I am socially inept in situations like this where everybody but me seems aware of usual and customary traditions. At my own wedding, I'd never heard of the silly thing with the intertwined punch cups at the wedding cake until the very moment I was suppose to perform this contortion myself. I thought surely they were kidding. Who comes up with this stuff?

At our son's wedding, the mother of the groom will do something with a candle, lighting one, extinguishing another, I think, and will sit in the first seat, right (or is it left?) side of the center aisle. I guess I should just find her and sit beside her. I'll go where they point me.

Oh wow, look. Here's Nate on stage at his high school commencement, singing a song he wrote for the event. Remember? He had the audience in the palm of his hand. There are more: here, he's twenty-one, muscular and tan after walking down the back roads of a bunch of eastern states from Bar Harbor, Maine to arrive three months later on Goose Creek. Now that little escapade put some gray hairs on our heads, for sure, didn't it? And this snapshot is from the semester he spent in Belfast and then worked on the dairy farm in the Alps. My, my—our world traveler.

If our children must live far away, we're happy they have at least chosen nice places for us to visit. Soon, he'll head back to Vancouver for another few years until he graduates. Where in the world he and the new missus will end up, of course, only God knows. And He has known—since Nate was small: our boy has belonged only partly to us, and to the world and to God. We've been setting him free over and over all his life to do whatever his life is meant to do. This wedding will be only one more letting go along that path.

So we will send young man and wife off on their honeymoon and come home from Missouri, pick up the dog, get the

wood stove warming the house again, and tidy up the place quickly because we have company coming. You see, we live in a pretty nice place to visit too, and the newlyweds will be in our home—and still his home—with us on Goose Creek a few days for Christmas. And I must be sure and take plenty of pictures.

In Sickness and In Health
For the Time, Being

If a spouse was to keep a book of petty gripes and minor grievances over the course of a long marriage, what interesting reading it would make, don't you think? I have one more addition to my own growing tome, see if you don't agree it deserves an entry.

It was barely 4 a.m. I'm not sure I'd even had coffee.

SNAP! A loud noise and simultaneous white flash of pain and terror shocked my brain like the blast wave of an explosion, so much more so because I was simply walking down the two steps from the dining room into the cold, dark front room lit only by the coals of the past night's fire in the wood stove.

What the H___ was that! My mind recoiled in fear and agony that came so suddenly with no warning. I waved my throbbing fingertip in the air as if to put out a fire.

"Sorry" she said meekly from her cereal bowl in the next room.

"You did WHAT!?" I couldn't believe what I was hearing.

"I found it upstairs in the back room and didn't know what to do with it, so I put it on the stair post where you'd see it last night."

I hadn't seen it, complete with a smear of peanut butter: a cocked mousetrap.

I rest my case.

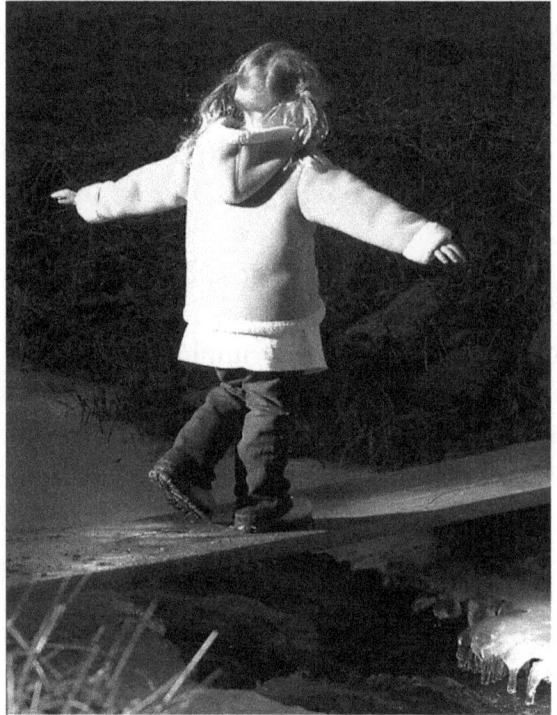

She was ahead of us and in the middle of the icy "balance beam" board across the icy creek before we knew it—going slowly, minding her steps, and safe enough. Her body knew without study the physics of balance, her arms like outriggers lifted to fine tune each step placed in the exact center of the board.

6

Early Physics
Curious By Nature

Have you ever shown your kids the scar on your elbow where you fell out of the apple tree at granny's when you were ten, or the one on your shin from when the grapevine broke while it was your turn to swing out over the gully? Scrapes and bruises of childhood were the merit badges for what you learned about physics outdoors.

A vacant lot or patch of woods or pasture was an outdoor classroom, and without knowing it, you discovered gravity and friction, velocity and momentum. You took the measure of the power of your arms and the spring in your legs. You learned with great precision how fast you must accelerate to make it across in "jump the ditch."

Lessons of trajectory and ballistics I learned from rocks. I skipped them across ponds, threw them with increasing accuracy and velocity at empty cans or fence posts and heaved big ones kersplash into puddles. I even made a rock-hurling sling one Sunday after hearing at church about what David did to the Giant. And I learned the hard way about centrifugal force and the fact that a boy's early practice in giant-slaying should only happen far enough away from the nearest windows!

The pleasure and joy and exhilaration of exploring wild places, of discovering the potential of your own wit and strength and new skills outside far outweighed anything that ever required a band-aid. Am I right?

It's hard to let them go out there equipped with only their energy, curiosity and naïve clumsiness. They will sometimes, as they grow stronger and more skilled, bring home the kind of bumps and bruises we gladly suffered as children. But try to give them reasonable freedom as they play outdoors, especially in "unimproved" natural settings. We owe them the right to explore and learn from the rough edges of a place on their own terms. Didn't you?

* She was ahead of us and in the middle of the icy "balance beam" board across the icy creek before we knew it—going slowly, minding her steps, and safe enough. Her body knew without study the physics of balance, her arms like outriggers lifted to fine tune each step placed in the exact center of the board.

* Can you hear the questions Abby is asking: Is this dangerous? Am I brave enough to do this? What will happen if I fall? How slow should I go to make it across? And once on the other side: the thrill of success, the confidence of a challenge faced and overcome.

* Am I a negligent grandfather because I stopped to focus my lens on granddaughter Abby crossing the slippery foot bridge rather than running frantically to protect her? What's a photographer grampa to do?

* "Be careful!" heard too often might make a child hesitant to try something new or investigate an intriguing new place. Would words like "pay attention" or "use good judgment" be better, and give them a heads-up without undue fear?

Seeds of Doubt: Crime Scene Biologist
Earth Companions

I was twenty-seven years old, and new to the Biology faculty at the community college. I had quickly become known as the "hippie teacher" since I alone among my older colleagues had hair just over my collar and wore little John Lennon glasses perched on my nose. But more than that, I was frequently seen around the county with my entourage of tree-hugging students who had signed up for my Field Botany class.

We were quite conspicuous as we scoured the roadsides and fields for new and wonderful plants to identify and admire, photograph, or consume in a 'wild foods' dish. But my reputation as a stalker of wildflowers and salamanders lead to two opportunities for medical sleuthing I really wasn't prepared for.

One mid-summer evening, the phone rang. It was the police. They were calling from the hospital regarding the identification of a plant substance associated with a possible poisoning. They wanted to know if I could help them identify the plant source from the seeds they found in the pockets of the young man who was now hallucinating in the emergency room.

"Yea, right!" I thought to myself. There is no Petersons Field Guide to Spores and Seeds. But I told them "I am on my way, though I'm not sure I will be able to help you."

"This is urgent," they said. "Hurry!"

When I arrived at the community hospital, a very thin teenage boy lay under a sheet in the ER, writhing and ashen, with accelerated heart rate and profuse sweating. And he was gorked out of his ever-lovin' head—trippin' right near the edge, man. And in his pocket was a vial of seeds. The logical assumption was that many more of them were in his gut, sending substances unknown to what was left of his brain. Depending on what the active property was, pending identification, a decision would need to be made right away to pump his stomach, induce vomiting, or start administering the appropriate antidote.

I assumed the role of TV Crime Scene Investigator. I poured the seeds from the vial into a stainless steel basin under bright examination lights. Tight-lipped, with the occasional inquisitive grunt or knowing mutter, I prodded at the seeds. Holding one with a pair of hemostats, I scraped it expertly with a scalpel (for no real purpose other than for dramatic effect), then sat silently for a pregnant moment as the tension grew. Against all odds, I had an answer for the police, nurses and doctors tensely waiting around the edges of the room.

I had the answer! Dear lord, what were the chances that I could have identified a SEED! But the distinctive, thick, kidney-shaped seeds of Jimson Weed were like no others. Case solved. Possible outcome without prompt intervention: death.

This boy was lucky, if stupid. Start the stomach pump, administer physostig-
mine, call the kid's parents. And when he's able to stand up in a day or two, resist
the temptation to kick his backside for this fool's stunt. It was almost his last.

A few weeks later that same summer, I got another call at home, this time from
a distraught doctor. His two-year-old daughter had been entertaining herself in
the yard picking and apparently eating something out of the grass. When he went
to check on her, he discovered to his horror that there were many small, brown
mushrooms in the grass where she sat. Had the baby eaten any? Possibly many?
Were they poisonous? Should they pump her stomach—a traumatic thing for
anyone, much less a two-year-old?

Again, what did I know? There are dozens of small, nondescript brown lawn
mushroom species! This time, back in the same now-familiar hospital lab, I
made a quick spore print under a goose-neck lamp. Then I tapped some spores
onto a microscope slide and quickly adjusted the light and focus on the tiny
brown dots of the spores. There was no dramatic flourish this time since a
child's life might be at stake. But the answer wasn't long in coming.

"Okay. Here it is." I called the father over and read from *Mushrooms of North America* while he squinted into the microscope. "Gilled mushroom of lawns, peaked cap,
brown spores shaped like an apple pip: *Marasmius oreades*. Look here." I pointed to
the picture in the book as the anxious physician-father breathed a sigh of relief.

"Your daughter will be just fine, doc" I said. "And as a matter of fact, your little
girl has very good taste. These mushrooms are described in the field guide as
'edible, choice.' You can go home and have them in your spaghetti."

And as theme music fades slowly, the camera pans to follow the young nature-
sleuth, the thankful parents and the small mycophagous toddler as they walk
amiably together, away from the camera, into the sun, out the sliding doors of
the dimly-lit hospital waiting room.

Ravens on Buffalo
Earth Companions

A cold front had come through the day before our autumn hike to the top of Buffalo Mountain, the bare-backed crest of our county's highest elevation. Temperatures would be crisp but not cold. The humidity was low so visibility would reach to the farthest horizon. What a great day to be on that high spine of rock with friends, near the peak of the leaf color change!

But the wind gauges from Blacksburg showed a constant gale of thirty mph with higher gusts—and it would be even worse at almost four thousand feet of the bare windswept 4000 foot summit—brutal, with chills in the thirties. We'd dress for fall at the bottom and winter at the top of our hike. Ann had never been up, and I wanted it to be a good experience for her. She's no sissy, but I've been miserable on that mountain more than once.

By the time we reached the first open glade at the crest, the temperature was pleasant, and the wind blew mostly over us rather than at us, but the calm was to be short-lived. We turned through the obligatory 360 degree survey of the horizon as one feels compelled to do at the top, and before us, a clear horizon thirty to seventy miles away. We took our bearings, soaking it all in.

Through binoculars we could pick out the tallest buildings in Winston-Salem and Greensboro. Pilot Mountain's distinctive bald head rose strikingly to the south. I pointed out to Ann the white ball of the NEXRAD tower on Coles Knob, visible without the binoculars, on the west horizon just a mile from the headwaters of Goose Creek.

Even though I'd carried my camera bag and tripod to the top, my photographic expectations were low. The cloudless sky offered little interest; the colors were surprisingly subdued a week short of peak, and we'd have to leave before the late afternoon lighting began to add shadows and pictorial interest to the scenes below. And then we heard the sound that changed everything.

"Raven!" I said immediately, though it came from behind me. My friend spotted them through the binoculars just beyond the steepest end of the mountain—the head and shoulders of the resting buffalo. There were five black birds.

"I think they're crows" he replied, as I shielded my eyes to watch them rise and fall in the wind that had by then risen in gusts to 30 mph hard out of the north.

"I'll admit I've never seen more than two ravens together in the same place at the same time, and those birds may be crows, but what I heard was definitely a raven" I said with absolute confidence; we hear ravens almost every day at home, and I know that familiar hoarse "rawwwk."

These black birds were larger and far more acrobatic than common crows we thought them at first to be. They were obviously enjoying one another's company. Forgive my attribution of human emotions to other kinds of creatures, but I don't think this is entirely in error in this instance, nor would you, had you seen the joy we witnessed in this performance.

Our friends were first to notice as we stood on the highest point of the mountain, our daypacks resting on top of the metal rod that benchmarked the spot for map-makers. "One of them is carrying something" and the rest of us trained our eyes on the lead bird. I stood up for a photograph with my 200 mm lens—about half of the power I would have preferred to close the distance on this swift, black subject. A gust of north wind pushed me back down on my haunches.

The raven that carried the dark object was "it" and the others gave chase—usually from below, in case the lead bird were to drop the parcel. I imagined this was a rule of their game: I drop it. You catch it. Five minutes later, a bird appeared with a conspicuous white something, first in its beak, then in its talons. The object had indistinct edges, a downy white feather was my guess. Again, at least one more bird pursued the carrier. If birds know play, we saw it on the Buffalo that day.

To watch their rolls and tumbles, spins and dives gave a belly rush, as if it were we who were hurtling through space. We watched them find the path of stronger currents in the constant thirty mile an hour north winds as clearly as we find a marked trail in forest. They entered those rivers of air with the timing and agility of a surfer taking the best wave.

First one bird, then the next rode turbulent tubes of wind up the rocky notch below us. At the head of the ravine each surfer lifted at the still point, hovered briefly, and fell with wings pulled tight, disappearing below our line of sight, only to reappear when it was his turn again.

We watched enthralled until our faces and fingers went numb from the cold wind. But the ravens did not feel the cold, or know the fear of heights or sense the risk of hurtling at great speed toward rock walls. They reveled in their medium and in their time together, and for a giddy once-in-a-lifetime moment, we were able to ride the currents with them.

Please Santa! No New Clothes for Christmas
Within Our Means

Our guests asked for a tour of our house after dinner. As we walked through the downstairs, I mentioned that the closets were added in our renovation of the place in 1999.

"Houses just didn't have closets back in the 1870s," I explained. Of course this wasn't a new revelation, but the significance of that fact began to take on a new relevance the more I considered why closets have become as essential to our homes today as indoor plumbing.

The generation that built this house designed it to fit their needs, and they just didn't need closets. With only two or three sets of clothes per person at any given time, their entire wardrobe could easily hang in an armoire or be stored neatly folded in a chest-of-drawers.

I pulled open the bi-fold doors of my side of the closet and surveyed a multi-colored hanging landscape of cloth—at least one shirt for every day of the month and half as many pairs of slacks. The metal bar sagged under their combined weight.

Like you, I try to be vigilant about personal health by not eating too much, and I'm trying to be more conscious of the planetary costs of eating foods transported a thousand miles or more to our table. But in my closet epiphany I realized that I had been oblivious to these same concerns about the ultimate costs—personal and global—of clothing gluttony.

My scant six feet of closet bar represents the tiniest fraction of the $282 billion spent on clothing every year in this country—the second largest consumer sector after food. Consider that most homes built in recent years have one or more walk-in closets the size of our grandparent's bedrooms!

While clothes became 25% cheaper from 1992 to 2002 (as more and more was imported from places other than our own once-local textile factories) our buying of clothing in all its forms surged disproportionately by more than 75% during this same period!

Yes, clothing has really become a great bargain. Or has it? What do your rainbow selections of blouses and accessorized sweaters actually cost the earth? Let's pull just one surprising thread in this complex, unsustainable clothing conundrum, and see where it leads.

Consider good ol' cotton. What's not to like? It's a natural fiber—soft, warm to the touch, a renewable resource (as compared to petroleum-derived synthetic fibers like polyester and nylon.) We like cotton close to us, touching our skin in the form of undies and jammies and such. Yes sir, it feels good.

But consider these facts for the non-organically-produced product: "Cotton accounts for one of every four pounds of pesticides sprayed on U.S. farmland. Almost twenty-two billion pounds of weed killer are applied annually to U.S.

cotton—more chemical per acre than is sprayed on soybeans and three times as much as for an acre of wheat.

Bleaching the cloth for a single shirt generates as much as fifteen gallons of polluted wastewater. Environmental costs are even worse for Chinese-manufactured cotton garments. And just try to find an item of apparel these days that isn't made there.

In the Christmas rush, we grab up armloads of inexpensive (if not, in the final accounting, cheap) disposable and fleetingly-fashionable apparel for gifts even as we sense that somehow in this global economy, our bargain benefit is likely a trade-off for another world community's costly loss.

Wal-Mart CEO Lee Scott defends his store's enormous lowest-bidder import of textiles: "Our customers simply don't have the money to buy basic necessities between paychecks." But someone has pointed out that "maintaining a regime of ecologically unsustainable but low prices in order to sustain purchasing power for the poor solves a problem for a subset of the population but reproduces another one for the entire planet."

This throws that Big Box Store's current slogan into question: Spend Less. Live Better.

Better for who or what and for how long? Closets at Christmas are good places to sit and think about that spin. And I'm pretty sure that Buy Less, Live Better wasn't even close to the encouragement the purveyors of stuff had in mind for us as Christmas shoppers.

So in this season of giving and getting, feasting and celebrating, we give thanks that we have the basic necessities of ample food and clothing to live warm and healthy lives. And we ask for the wisdom to know when to push back from the table and say we have had enough.

Carolina Bays: An Earth Mystery
Not Fish Nor Fowl

From my virtual vantage point thirty miles above the swamp forests and sandy flats of the South Carolina coastal plain, I navigate Google Earth along and well to either side of our anticipated travels from Goose Creek to the doorstep of some Floyd friends who still live part time in Conway near Myrtle Beach.

For me, getting map routes ready for a trip like this is about as much of the joy of the journey as the travel itself. And here, I was exploring both new and known country.

Below me was a landscape familiar and comfortable, little different from the coastal plain of Mississippi where my wife grew up and where we often visited after the kids came along. The land I watched passing below me would be saturated for a good bit of the year, the water table very close to the surface.

So it surprised me to see to what extent coastal Carolina has turned the too-wet pine pocosins and savannahs into tract housing and strip malls, apparent even from many miles in space.

But what puzzled me most in "flying" over this area for the first time were the oblong shapes imprinted in the ground. The ones I noticed first were labeled on the map as "Pee Dee Islands." Though the Pee Dee is a river, these so-called islands were waterless, egg-shaped, the largest a mile long and three fourths as wide.

The more I explored along the coastal plane of both South and North Carolina, the more of these odd rimmed areas I could clearly see. Some cover only a few acres, most green with vegetation. Some (the largest being 7-mile-long Lake Waccamaw in North Carolina) are filled with water.

A great many of the larger ones are oval in shape, slightly elongated along a North-west to South-east axis. In places, they partially or almost completely

overlap each other, sprayed by an invisible wind dropping so many giant drop-
lets against cypress swamp or lowland forest. What is going on here?

I am by no means the first to wonder about this. The elliptical shapes and vast
distribution of these earth forms, now known as "Carolina Bays" were not
appreciated until 1933 when the first aerial photos of the area brought this
oddity back for study.

Extending from southern New Jersey to northern Florida, there are at least 500,000
such elliptical depressions—called bays because of the shrub and tree species that
typically fill them, and so distinctive from surrounding land that they are indeed
often called islands. You can download a Google Earth overlay that outlines vast
numbers of them from several counties in North Carolina, but they are clearly
visible without such assistance. Just look south of Fayetteville on Google Earth.
There are also some more recently discovered bays near Midlothian in Virginia.

So surely, seventy five years after their discovery, we must know why they exist
and how and when they were formed. No, as a matter of fact, we don't. The
explanations of causes fall into two main camps: terrestrial and extra-terrestrial.
Both have arguments in favor, both lack the "smoking gun" to say with certainty
that the case is closed.

While the theory isn't fully substantiated by any means, I find most interesting
the explanation that an air-burst cometary explosion splashed these half million
bays onto the landscape, but no meteorite fragments are found below them.

The closest and most notable air-burst event in historical times is the Tunguska
phenomenon over Siberia in 1908. Trees were scorched and blown down over
a thirty mile radius, but as with the Carolina bays, no meteor material was ever
found. A similar mid-air explosion or earth impact may explain the geologically
sudden Ice Age disappearance (about 13,000 years ago) of previously abundant
large mammals like the mammoth (some instantly freeze-dried with food still
in their mouths.)

Based on dating of the sediments in some of them, the Carolina Bays may have been formed at this time of world-wide cataclysm. Or they might have formed more gradually from natural processes of wind and groundwater, dune and ocean currents. The jury is very much undecided, while anyone can now see the evidence.

While the Phoenix lander probes the Angry Red Planet for answers, I encourage you to take a look for yourself at a mystery a little closer to home. [Search Carolina bays online!]

Floyd County Airspace: a Busy Place!
Local Color

The power company man stopped by the house to tell us a low-flying helicopter would be in the area over the next few days, trimming the power line right-of-way with the world's largest power saw, down here at what he described wryly as "the end of the line," electrically-speaking.

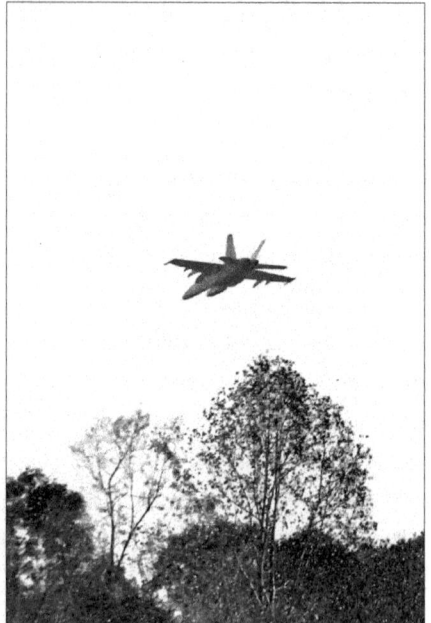

I heard the drone of whirring rotors and spinning blades for hours that morning. The motors throw their voices, echoing between ridges, and I was never able to fix exactly where on the compass the combination of craft and saw was working.

Then suddenly the noisy combo rose from behind the pines and settled within view of our front porch to finish the work the Asplundh crew had started a few months ago—clearing the line that crosses Goose Creek Run down at the low-water bridge.

End of the line, indeed. Given the sparsely-settled and rugged terrain of this northeastern slope of the Great Valley near the edge of the county, we are often the first to lose power, and the last to get it back. We wished our tree-trimming visitors the best of success towards our sustained winter power, and if their unusual tools would get the job done, bring it on.

The saw you see here is one of five operated by Aerial Solutions of Tabor City, NC. There isn't a lot of info out there about the company or process, but what I gleaned from the web was helpful to explain what I was seeing in the airspace over Goose Creek.

In the inset, you can tell that this enormous saw consists of ten (or in some instances there may be up to as many as 15) 2-foot circular blades somehow guided with more or less precision along the margins of the forest where branches meets the clearing that contains the power lines. What keeps the whole thing from flailing wildly on hitting a knotty snag was quite beyond me. I had to see what I could learn, and here's the skinny:

The mechanism is driven by a 45 horsepower snowmobile motor at the top of the apparatus. The blades are belt driven, suspended from a semi-rigid aluminum shaft (hinged at the top of the saw and at the helicopter) that allows the saw rig to move front to back but reduces the tendency for it to spin on its axis or move laterally. This gives the pilot adequate control to avoid hitting the lines. (However, this seems to have happened on the second day of work, and we were offered a big "oops" by AEP when our power disappeared for several hours.)

The 825 pound tethered assembly (weight depends on how many blades) extends a total of 85 or more feet below the bottom of the helicopter. The pilot, watching out his door-less side skillfully tilts the craft so that its prop-wash will blow limbs into the path of the spinning blades. This mighty wind was evident as I watched from a safe distance, large trees blowing as if Hugo had come back to haunt our hills for an hour on a clear and otherwise calm day.

The helicopter pilot can release the whole saw mechanism in an emergency, and can land (usually in a field near the work site overnight) with the saw out on the ground in front of it.

I had put my camera on the back porch, ready to grab when the strange work came into view. So I was snapping away, fascinated by the nuanced expertise of the helicopter pilot. My mind was focused on the image in the viewfinder when a loud roar just overhead made me fear at first that there is about to be a terrible crash.

I pulled away from the camera to take in the larger picture of what was happening, and out of the corner of my eye, a dark shape zipped south. By the time I turned the lens towards it, the source of the roar—a military jet—had almost disappeared over the east ridge of our valley.

Had I been expecting it and had the lens zoomed back to take in a larger field of view, I probably could have caught both helicopter and fighter jet in the same frame—and they would not have been separated by much vertical distance at all!

Wouldn't you think the tree-trimmer folks would ask the Air Force folks to kindly find a different practice route on the days their helicopters plan to hover for hours at treetop level? Today, their rotors came dangerously close to the underside of fighter jets passing so low we could see the rivets on their wings!

My Woodlot in Life is Enough
Body and Soul Together

Half-jokingly I often say that the true measure of a man can be taken from the size, orderliness and contents of his woodpile.

If that is indeed the case, then I have in the past couple of years devolved to a brutish and slovenly derelict of our species. You see, I've taken to burning sissy wood—more on the order of glorified kindling than real wood with a manly heft to it.

Of course I'm in as much need as ever for the heat that comes from the wood I cut—and my wife, it seems, gets more cold-natured every winter. But the putting by of four cords that we burn over six months each year becomes more of a chore faced with a certain dread than the pleasure it used to be before I woke up with 60 year old joints and muscles.

The job can still be done, mind you, and I still have the desire to do it. But on this rugged land, the effort to cut "body wood" of any real size is both more difficult and more risky than truckloads in other places and decades past.

My reluctance comes from this lay of the land, geographic and orthopedic, coupled with a new unwillingness to vie for the Darwin Award I almost won posthumously last year with a near miss from a felled tree whose path of fall I severely misjudged.

So what I have found is that we can still bring home truckloads of wood from the few acres we have access to along Nameless Creek but we can't make it happen only from what windfall and decay offer us. We'll have to cut live and standing shrubbery—a term I'll use because honestly, the object of our chain saw this year could hardly be called "timber."

And herein is my enthusiasm and rationale for a sissy woodpile: a pound of wood is a pound of wood. As I understand it, the BTU capacity of the different wood species comes more from their relative density than from any inherent differences of energy storage in the wood itself. It takes twice the poplar, say, to produce x units of heat because it is half as dense as something like oak. But wood burns at a given rate of heat yield, species compared pound for pound and at the same moisture level.

You will find all kinds of hardwood species rated for BTU's on a by-the-cord basis: oak and hickory, locust and cherry. But you will not find our wood du jour that makes up the stacks for next winter: spicebush and witch hazel.

Both are considered shrubs or small trees—spicebush, growing wrist-sized trunks of 8 to 15 feet and witch hazel, smooth calf-sized trunks of equal length. They grow in abundance along the creek bank, splaying toward the horizontal as their multiple trunks gain size in the soft sandy soil. They are safe to drop, easy to carry and both about as dense in my hands as hickory.

This new way of doing things has got me to thinking. The old timers say that the best kind of wood to burn is the kind of wood you have at hand. There's a certain kind of wisdom in this that reaches beyond the choices we've made in the woodlot.

Soon, perhaps this old-fashioned living-within-one's-means way of thinking about resources will be commonplace and post-modern progressive: meeting our needs from what we have so that we have what we need. It's just common sense in the absence of cheap oil.

The best kind of (fill in the blank: salad greens and wooden bowl, wine, soap or knitting yarn) is what we have at hand locally and can get with relative efficiency, with the least possible depletion or risk to the source that provides it, and is a thing that can be produced in such a way that the source keeps on giving for the long term to those who consume from it.

So I'm really not so apologetic for my wimpy woodpile. Let's just say that I have a new vision for what's enough and ways to appreciate and use what I already have. Along with millions of others in this Post Peak world, I'm exploring options to sustain my own demand for natural resources—even though my grip is not what it once was—out of what lies within my local grasp.

Assaulted and Battered
(Yet More Beeping in Paradise!)
Within These Walls

"Beep." I pretended I didn't hear it. "Beep!" the shrill cry insisted. Maybe it will just go away. "BEEP!!!" and by that time the dog had heard it too, his quivering body pressed up against my office chair so hard that he knocked my hands off the keyboard.

It was 9:00, our usual bedtime and a weekend, to boot. Why do household crises so often coincide with late nights, weekends—and holidays!

The dog, in his neurotic way, becomes agitated and frantic to get out the door when things go beep inside. Perhaps he was assaulted by a kitchen timer as a small puppy. We've considered therapy. We sent him to the outdoor pen while we problem-solved, with the thought that we might be joining him there later if we couldn't silence the source of his and now our vexation.

Something had to be done or none of us, man nor beast, would get any sleep. The sound came from upstairs, and was, I knew right away, the fire alarm in the hallway. I had taken the battery out a couple of months back when the 9 volt went bad and the dog had beep-freaked on us. (The battery backup insures the alarm works even if house current is off.) Now, here it was mysteriously beeping again–possessed by some strange power, even without the battery!

BEEP! Great Caesar's Ghost! Now the one in the bedroom was beeping too! The condition was spreading; this called for more serious measures.

So I unscrewed the alarm units from the ceiling mounts and disconnected them entirely. There! Severed at the neck. That should do the trick.

BEEP! AGGGGHHH! It was like being screamed at by a decapitated head! Both units lay on the hallway shelf and continued to beep from their ceiling connectors!

Ramp it up a notch: we were about to go to bed anyway, so I'd just turn off the power to the upstairs. Quick! To the breaker box, Batman!

Switches off, and the upstairs is dark. But NO! The zombie alarms could not be killed. This is weirding me out, man. So at 9:15, I scraped ice off the windshield of the Subaru and headed off to the first convenience store that had batteries. Convenience, by the way, is a relative term, and a misnomer when you live where we live and the stores live where they live.

The closest would be fifteen miles one way. And the ultimate terror: replacing the batteries will make no difference when I get home with them. Google the closest Motel 6.

So, despite one large buck who threw himself in front of the car, and a very small fox who was standing in the middle of the road on one of five blind curves before you get to the hardtop and countless other suicidal reflective eyes just off the shoulders of the winding road down Allegheny Spring Road, I found three 9 volt batteries in Shawsville. Now what?

Finally: I'm home just before 10, sleepy, bewildered, and anxious. It is the moment of truth. The dog listens anxiously from his sanctuary in the cold dark of his alfresco housing. The shrieking from inside stops. And they all live happily ever after (with a surplus of 9 volt batteries on hand)—at least until the next haunting by that Thing That Goes Beep in the Night.

Driveway Moment: Blackbirds on Goose Creek
For the Time, Being

It is my favorite short stretch of the four miles of our slow road home, a place where, on the topo the contours converge from both sides, creek and road lie close together, side by side.

Just here, as you round the bend, the road lifts a dozen feet above the creek for the sole purpose, I like to imagine, of giving rise to lofty thoughts that come from an elevated views of things. Another hundred yards towards the house and the creek flows only a foot or two lower than the gravel road once more.

The old hemlocks—what remains of them—stand tall and close here, dark-brooding over rhododendrons. Only during the middle daylit hours, slanting sun finds the notch in the south ridge, and floods this green sanctuary with shafts of glory. At its brightest, this is the Dappled Lane.

Rhythms slow and calm at just this spot on the return trip home. But wait! What is all the commotion here today, motion and noise in this still-life watercolor? Eyes and mind struggle to comprehend the story. An unexpected drama unfolds in dazzling sunlit ground and tree branch and the deepest daytime shadows.

Animated slips of silver and black, of night and day, dart low across the road in front of me, shoot up into the branches from all sides, plunge toward the shallow water of Goose Creek.

Grackles—a fall-like flock of them gregarious and jostling about in forest in July? It seems that the water—what little remains of the creek this summer, no deeper than a songbird's knees—that is the source of their excitement.

I pull the car to the side of the road, ten feet higher and twenty feet from the stream, and stop the engine. Sleek black birds reel and flash silver-white in the streaming sun, then as quickly vanish into the shadows, laughing.

In the sunlit amber water of the creek, a dozen or more birds dip and splash in a single pool, then fluff and preen on the rocky banks. Each one in turn wades back in again and again, undisturbed as I watched. Overhead under the canopy, dozens more creak and yip softly—joyously I'll venture—while more waiting their turn in the bath. They scratch in the soft duff of last year's leaves among tall back-lit wood ferns.

As much as I enjoy my times in the garden, my excursions to town or even some hours at work, it is this kind of unbidden, unexpected serendipitous gift of a moment in nature that makes me smile when I look back and remember.

And I will remember. I regretted not having a camera with me; but there are other ways to take pictures for our book of days.

My twenty-first century face appeared for real in the mirror that millennial year,
no puckering required, pleated by laugh lines and crow's feet, full of wonder, creased
like my old first baseman's glove. It was the face of a Lost Boy, riding time like a
pair of skates, surfing its glassy surface to the vanishing point, standing still yet
moving moment by precious moment through time, aging, after all.

7

What They Hold In Their Hands
Curious By Nature

I grew up watching television's Wild Kingdom and Disney's re-enacted depictions of nature. To a young boy of the times, those dramatized caricatures of what goes on in the living world of animals and plants were extraordinary. How much more dazzling then are the visual encounters of nature available to today's audience of virtual field trippers. While there's much to be learned from sophisticated digital visits to exotic landscapes, there is also a price: this second-hand proximity has become as close as many of us feel we need to get to the natural world.

Vicariously through the monitor screen, you are a spectator in the bleachers, an inert watcher separated from the Reality Show of nature as it exists beyond your walls. When the feature is over, you've been entertained, but you haven't been changed. Your boots never get dirty.

Seeing nature through screen-media is no substitute for touching, smelling, feeling; for being a participant in the learning space. As they say, the map is not the territory.

I encourage you—parents, grandparents, older siblings— to get up from your entertainment center and take the children in your life out into the territory of the real world beyond the screen door. Learn with them to be amazed by earth's wonderfully-real stage and the creature-characters around you every hour.

Get out into the where of your life, into the soil and oxygen of your own nature drama. And if you can teach your eyes and your children's to see them, the ordinaries close to home can be remarkably full of discovery, satisfaction and life lessons. (But you probably remember this, don't you, from your own childhood?)

Take your young charges off the leash of your apprehension and excess of caution. Use good judgment on their behalf of course. Pay attention, and know the real dangers, far fewer than our greatest media-stoked fears. Then let them go—to be changed by what they experience by touch and sight.

Hands-on, let them handle nature in their own way, with their own hands. Create a safe space for them to learn what the real world feels like—to know the tough-spongy texture of a mushroom. To feel the life pulsing inside the shell of a box turtle's cold hard carapace. To feel the tickle of a millipede's "thousand feet" crawling on the back of their hand, or know the touch of the red-spotted newt moving on his short legs by wiggling his body in an S-curve left and right against their palm.

What they hold in their hands today—iPod or millipede—can make all the difference in where their center of importance will be in their adult lives. Think about it.

The Demise of the Eastern Hemlock
Earth Companions

"Sadly, we've not yet seen the first black throated blue warblers this year, and I'm afraid they will become more and more uncommon as our once magnificent darkest green hemlock trees succumb to the insect called the wooly adelgid. Our hillsides were once covered with the dark dropping branches of hemlock— my favorite tree. Now they stand gaunt and gray, sad skeletons with bony arms uplifted, frozen in a final unanswered prayer." —from *Slow Road Home*

Eastern hemlock (Tsuga canadense, by all means not to be confused with Socrates' poison—another plant entirely) became my favorite tree after I first knew it from the Bankhead Wilderness in northern Alabama long ago. It has since become a familiar marker of those places where I feel most at home in this world.

When we moved to Goose Creek in 1999, our hillsides and ridges were dark green with hemlocks. Only a few years later, our trees sickened like the rest of the eastern forest hemlock die-off, doomed to suffer a slow but certain death. The cause: the Hemlock Wooly Adelgid (pronounced "ah del jid"), an imported scale insect that sucks the life out of our hemlocks. The adelgid is an invasive with no natural predators to check its spread.

These insects look like tiny cottony masses and you'll see them—should you find a hemlock that still clings to life—on the underside of the needles of this evergreen tree. While individual trees may be successfully protected in several ways by direct application of insecticides— should you be so inclined—so far, nothing has promised to save the day for them in real forests.

Imagine: an entire species disappearing before our eyes. But of course, this kind of extinction is happening invisibly and at an alarming rate across the planet. More often than not, the disappearance of plant and animal species is due to a single invading alien: us. As there are more of us, and we travel between continents transporting spores and seeds; as we clear land for roads and shopping centers; as we burn acid-producing coal to satisfy our appetite for electricity—we become agents of extinction.

But if we have eyes to see, if we know our trees as fellow-creatures, value what they do in their silence and will become their voice, perhaps this species—and so many others like American chestnut—will be back in the forest canopy for our children's children.

Snake in the Grass
Earth Companions

The energized air of utterly clear, crisp days of October makes a fella want to find something to do outdoors. By that time of year, the woodpile needs tending, and the garden, long gone by, needs only a few more final acts of closure to see it through until spring. The leaves have reached their autumn glory and begun to fall, so leaf-raking just outside the back door is a great pick-up job that lasts for weeks, a fine escape when the wife is in a cleaning frenzy inside.

Just behind the house, I knelt beside the shed to toss aside a flat rock. With it moved aside, I could rake a clean slate of the gravel pad in the shelter of the roof overhand where we would stack a quarter-cord of firewood. To my delight, in the cool shade of that rock, in the midst of the reds and yellows of autumn coiled a brilliant green six-inch snake!

I gave up a WHOOP! like a miner who'd discovered gold. (My wife's quite used to this, and she knows better than to expect precious minerals.) We'd seen two eighteen-inch adult green snakes here in the six years on Goose Creek—only two. With their emerald disguise, they are notoriously hard to see in the summer grass and low bushes where they hang out. But also they are increasingly rare. As insect-eaters, their populations have taken a nose-dive in locked step with the number of acres cleared for agriculture, housing and commerce and with the millions of gallons of pesticides used.

This six-inch juvenile was sluggish, having already bedded down for the cold months, only to be exposed suddenly to the warm afternoon sun. The wildlife paparazzi of Goose Creek tormented him for a few minutes with their cameras. Then he was gently restored to his spot next to the shed. Every time I brought in an arm load of wood to the stack, I'd imagine him coiled cozily in the chilly dark of his hiding place, dreaming of crickets.

The word "snake" is associated with danger, death and evil. Maybe it goes back in our culture to the Garden of Eden story. And there are dangers, to be sure, just as there are from individuals of our own species. But there are also small, harmless snakes, too small and passive to strike. Don't harbor (or share) the idea that the only good snake is a dead one. Remember: your children are watching!

Your Favorite Mountaintop a Valley Fills
Within Our Means

Bulonium is fiction. Mountaintop removal is not. This is a little edgy, but I feel it needs to be here. In writing it, my aim was to awaken reader imaginations of what it would feel like if it was their mountains and scenic vistas and forests going into massive metal scoups, and bull-dozed into low places like our Goose Creek valley. This is an exercise. Or it is an alarm call. Our fictional bulonium is West Virginia's coal from real former mountains, its waste now obliterating real creeks and home places forever. Imagine.

You might as well learn about this it from me right here and now, because this is big news, and it will change everything about life in (your) County.

You probably haven't even heard of the rare element, balonium. But you will. It is needed for the manufacture of a certain kind of memory chip essential to the production of iPhones and the very top-selling computer games and certain in the recent generation of guided missiles used against evil doers. And here's the thing: (your) County is sitting on a mother load of it. But it won't be sitting anywhere much longer.

Balonium has been found throughout (your) County and parts of adjacent (name a couple of other) Counties in a three to six inch layer that in most places lies precisely at (give a number of feet elevation appropriate to your county's geology; find this on a topo map) feet above sea level. So the plan, as I understand it, is to slice away everything—and I mean everything—above that elevation to extract the mineral so necessary to the economic well-being of (some in) our nation—and in the interest of national security, of course.

Now, there's good news and there's bad news in all this. For all those who maintain that we need jobs no matter what, this massive extraction over the next four years will indeed bring some jobs and revenue to the area, it's true, but not as many jobs or as much money as you might think.

A single bucket machine operator can remove a hundred tons of "overburden" in a single bite. He does the work once done by a hundred miners or more. But hey, you might just be that one. And even though it IS your land being mined into oblivion, most of that money, I'm sorry to say, won't go to you or your kids. Oh yeah, and that stuff in the giant bucket was once where you lived. You'll have to make other arrangements.

Now back to some specifics as I figure them. For everything we'll gain, all we'll lose in our county will be everything above 2500 feet. Get out your topo map to help envision this. The summit and a good bit of the flanks of (a familiar) Ridge and (a familiar) Knob, almost all of the (well known high scenic) area will be lost, to name just a sampling of what will soon become mere places in our memory. And before I go on, let me explain what is to become of this former mountaintop so that you can begin to make preparations.

Every bucket scoop will contain entire forests of trees, shrubs (lots and lots of Rhododendron, Flame Azalea, and Mountain Laurel) and most of your favorite wildflowers. (A favorite vista) will go in one of those scoops; I'm glad I got a few pictures to keep from there, before there's no there there.

Some bucket-loads will hold old barns, stone spring houses, ancient homesteads and every forest and high meadow trail that ever meant anything to you. But remember, this is for the good of the nation, so don't go getting all squishy and sentimental here.

I meant to tell you exactly what becomes of the stuff in that bucket. It is no longer the top of the mountain, and although it was everything to you, there isn't any use for it anymore. It is simply waste in the national mind. Since it came from a high place, this means there was a lower place nearby, and this is where the mountaintop will spend the rest of geological time.

It can't be helped that under every one of those "valley fills" will lie what was once one of our creeks. I'd suggest you start now taking pictures of (name at least a half dozen familiar creeks). The way I figure it, in the interest of the national good, we'll lose some 62 miles of flowing water in our county alone. But it's just water; think how many bottles of it (your local grocery store) will sell when our wells no longer are fed by clean ground water that used to come from springs where there isn't any ground anymore.

But in spite of all these good things about the stripping away of our mountaintops, it does have its downside for those folks who were beginning to think that tourism could become a significant source of jobs and revenue in the county.

Of course the vistas from what will soon be the new "high places" at or below 2500 feet will not be something people take vacations here to look at. And our lazy crooked roads won't be quaint and peaceful any more, what with the day-and-night convoys of balonium-laden dump trucks rumbling out the new ambient hum of (your) County's future soundscape. That's progress.

Is this what-if imagined future far-fetched and impossible? Ask the folks in Kentucky and West Virginia if their lives—their forest, streams, roads, air, wells, and culture—have changed for the better since Mountain Top Removal (MTR) has come to take away their local balonium called coal.

Read this little thought exercise again. See it really happening. Put the mountains and creeks you love in the blanks. What does your gut tell you? Mine says this is the wrong way to do business. It's the wrong way to treat people and communities. And it says that MTR is a flagrant slap in the face of nature and of God. And if they were my mountains, I'd be writing pieces in my local paper to tell those who make these decisions about the fate of our precious land to find another way while there are still high places left to save.

FACT: Mountaintop removal has destroyed over 450 mountains and buried over 1,000 miles of streams throughout Appalachia, most in Eastern Kentucky and West Virginia.

Don't turn away. This IS our problem, too. Recommended reading online: ilovemountains.org

Conversion Experience from the Floyd Outback
Not Fish Nor Fowl

I wear a long face this week, reluctant to give ground. My wife has deemed that fifteen years with the same pair of bedroom slippers is long enough. A half-roll of shiny silver duct tape to hold the tops and soles together is just too whacky. She insists that I toss them. I know she's right. We'll see.

You should know that I bear this old-fashioned notion to buying and keeping: find a tool that works just right, a shirt that fits, a pair of slippers that know the shape of every bump and bunion. Stick with them like faithful friends until there's nothing left. Then patch and glue, wire and tape the thing together again; and use it a few more years. Toss away nothing lightly or too soon.

And so for me to be planning to abandon a perfectly functional if increasingly anemic four year old PC for a brand new Mac within the month is to break with my vow of 'til death do we part. What's more, this plan is a kind of voluntary divorce that disavows everything comfortable and familiar.

After more than twenty years of Windows PC devotion, this impending conversion carries the portent of a change of faith and normal habit. It will be like riding my horse backwards or wearing my slippers on my ears.

I will be for weeks—maybe months—awkward and fumbling in the new Promised Land, grumbling and inefficient, a lost soul unsure of a strange, new liturgy, not settled into the dogma of my new way of life. Waking up to a Mac on my desk that first morning will be to step out of the boat and walk on the water. The faithful tell me to keep my eye on the Great Apple.

Soon I'll wonder how I ever could have put faith in My Computer, have trusted Device Manager or sought direction from the duplicitous Start Button. I see it now, that hallelujah moment when I will hear nothing but the OS-X angels singing pure Truth.

But oh how I dread the purgatory that first must come—confronting the tangled web I've woven of cords and cables; facing the fear that perhaps I've sold my birthright for a faster CPU; confessing the powerlessness of a novitiate randomly dog-paddling about the shallow end of the learning pond. Fear no evil; this too shall pass.

To assuage my burden of guilt, the old PC, thankfully, won't go to the green box. It will live upstairs on my wife's desk, thus avoiding the issue of how to responsibly dispose of the remains of my obsolete hand-me-down, all the while predestined ultimately for the landfill.

And here, a confession: I intend to keep a foot in both camps—to be a technological chimera, a PresbyBuddhist, if you will. The new Mac processors will run both Windows and Mac software. So I can go to heaven AND come back as a Golden Retriever!

It's a difficult decision. I just know I don't want to go to Dell when I die. And come to think about it, when I take that last walk down those golden streets to my reward as my hard drive finally conks out, I think (don't tell my wife) I want to be wearing the tattered remnants of my duct-tape silver slippers.

Clean Hands: The Oldest New Idea
Not Fish Nor Fowl

Sometimes your mother was right. Cover your mouth when you sneeze. Wash your hands. Or else. Soap and water is the highest tech we need to prevent many illnesses.

Ignaz Semmelweis is hardly a house-hold name, but trust me: the practice that he recommended for hospital maternity wards more than a hundred and fifty years ago we have recently rediscovered as the single best way to prevent the spread of infectious disease: simple hand washing.

Semmelweis, a Hungarian obstetrician practicing in Vienna in the 1840s, made some critical discoveries that pointed toward the source of the alarmingly-high rate of maternal death caused by a mysterious "childbed (or puerperal) fever."

His first observation in 1844 was that, between the two wards in the same hospital where he lectured, one (staffed only by midwives) had a childbirth maternal death rate of just 2% while the other, staffed by medical students—who also performed autopsies—was 16%.

The hospital situation was so bad that the incidence of childbed fever symptoms was actually lower for women who had their babies unassisted on the streets of the city than for those whose children were born in the maternity wards of Vienna's prestigious hospital centers of medical research and education!

Things were so bad that just a year earlier, physician and author Oliver Wendell Holmes Sr. had said that "in my own family, I had rather that those I esteemed the most should be delivered unaided, in a stable, by the mangerside, than that they should receive the best help, in the fairest apartment, but exposed to the vapors of this pitiless disease."

This blame on malignant vapors must be forgiven, as it was some decades yet before Louis Pasteur would demonstrate conclusively that there are indeed invisible agents of infection we now know as bacteria. (Viruses would be discovered only much later.)

Simmelweis' claimed to his colleagues that he had proven a connection between childbed fever and the spread of "cadaverous particles." He further stated that doctors were the primary carriers of these particles from victim to victim, and that hand washing was the solution. As you might expect, this outrageous idea was ridiculed by pompous medical contemporaries. "Doctors are gentlemen, and gentlemen's hands are clean." Yeah, right.

I was thinking about all this a few weeks back as we made our way toward our next departure at the Chicago airport. I lifted my hand reflexively from the rail of (Caution! You are about to reach the end of the) moving walkway—a hand that by then had touched the touch of hands from across the country and around the world. Money, doorknobs, bathroom fixtures; runny noses, taxi cab seats, and moving handrails: my hand shared in the common contact and accumulated invisible microbial veneer left behind by a thousand washed and unwashed strangers.

We settled into seats and I got lost in my USA Today as our boarding time approached. I stopped myself at the last instant before I absentmindedly moistened my thumb with my mouth to turn the dry pages. Now there's a habit that would have Dr. Simmelweis screaming "cadaverous particles!"

So here we are in our modern, enlightened times on the other side of the age of the overworked miracle of antibiotics. We give these wee flightless, legless hitch-hikers (not only bacteria but also viruses, prions, fungi and protozoans) transportation around the world in a day, carry them far from the forests soils and remote mountain jungles where they evolved and where they do not so much harm outside their primate or mammalian or avian hosts.

Then too, we've saturated our cattle, chickens and children with penicillin and all its temporarily effective successors. By agricultural and medical overuse, we've managed to eliminate the susceptible bacterial strains and have left to survive those nasty variants that have managed to persist—even thrive—paradoxically and especially in hospitals where antibiotic use is the highest.

I emerged from the Travel Section of my newspaper for a last visit to the mens' room as our flight was called to board. It seemed especially noteworthy to me that there were no doors with handles to touch; soap and water and toilet-flushes happened without hands. And this time, I found something new: a quick, jet-powered dryer that you stick both hands into without touching. Infectious hands have achieved a new level of notoriety, it seems.

But even today, men are especially likely to neglect washing their hands in public rest rooms. And many folks mistakenly think that the alcohol-based dry washes or towelettes are as effective as a hand washing, or that the antibacterial soaps are a great advance over plain old soap and water. They aren't, and they may actually do harm: the use of antibacterials "may cause some bacteria to become resistant to commonly used drugs such as amoxicillin, the researchers say."

Even if you wash as frequently as you should, almost nobody washes for long enough. The Center for Communicable Disease recommends that you wash for at least 20 seconds. So how long is that? They suggest you wash your hands long enough by singing all the way through Happy Birthday, twice.

Now that little performance ought to get you some extra elbow room at the airport rest room sink, don't you think?

When A Tree Falls in the Forest
Body and Soul Together

It was a perfect winter day, brisk with high blue sky high above shredding low gray clouds. Nathan and I cut a load of firewood from the banks of Nameless Creek—as a good an excuse as any to spend an hour together during his short visit. Soon he would return to Missouri and home.

With the job done and as we prepared to go, I spotted a branchless cherry snag. It would drop easily and yield a few days' worth of heat next winter. Ten inches at the base and broken off abruptly fifteen feet up the trunk, it leaned out over the meadow some ten feet up the steep bank.

This would be an awkward cut, especially for notching the downhill side. The slope was deep in leaves. I certainly didn't want to go sliding down the hill holding a spinning chain saw in my hands. So contrary to my better judgment, I opted to just cut through the leaning trunk on the uphill side and let the weight of the tree finish the job. Bad idea.

With the bar half way through the diameter of the tree, the cut began to open on the uphill side. Another half inch, the tree was noticeably beginning to tip toward the floor of the open woods. I considered my path of escape, but on the steep slope and with the saw in my hands, I wouldn't be able to move quickly, but no matter: this little chunk of tree would pose no hazard. What could go wrong?

Another half inch, and the velocity of motion increased. I shut off the saw and began to move to the left. But just here the tree dance took an odd turn. A six foot slab of the downhill uncut third of the tree stood firm. It became a see-saw pivot point on which the remainder of the tree tipped. In this manner, as I watched in disbelief, the free portion of the tree trunk—easily 400 pounds of wood—careened steeply toward the ground, hitting first on its top.

And here, another surprise: there was far more resilience in this "dead" tree than I would have guessed because (still in slow motion) as the top struck the ground, it did not break. Instead the spring-loaded top threw the fallen body of the tree left and up the hill, its cut end landing higher up the bank than the stump from which it had been cut!

I reacted quickly and logically and moved left, paradoxically, into the path of the falling tree. Had I moved quicker in the "right" direction, I'd have been crushed.

A glancing blow threw me to the ground. "Dad! Are you alright?" Nathan asked, horrified. I answered "sure!" but thought I might be only dreaming I was still alive. It all happened so fast—in slow motion—if that makes any sense at all. And after a minute, I realized that only my left knee and ego were bruised.

Back home, we fetched the crutches from the attic, just in case. I never needed them. I am in much better shape than I have any right to be. I have four hundred pounds of that cherry split and stacked for next year. And I have a limp and a scar to remind me of how close to our own mortality we walk each day, even in our own back yards.

Can't Get There from Here
Within These Walls

We had a little adventure in the wee hours and are waiting for first light to show what last night's storm left us. For certain, our heavy board bridge across the creek is no longer there. How the dog got across the raging muddy water the first time is still a mystery.

"The dog wants out" she said about 2 o'clock, knowing it takes the least provocation to wake me from even the deepest sleep.

Tsuga stood beside the bed with is muzzle just inches from my face when I opened my eyes in the room, lit only by the battery-powered Christmas candle flickering its yellow light in our bedroom window. I rolled over, pretending I'd had a bad dream.

But there stood the dog, wagging his tail—a sure sign to me that he didn't have a full bladder. If he has to pee, he gets up from his bed in our bedroom and silently goes and stands by the back door. Somehow, I hear even this. No, he was up to no good and I could ignore him. But I couldn't ignore her.

Because it was raining hard before bedtime that night, she hadn't taken him out his usual last time, and now she felt guilty. "He really needs to go out now" she prodded both verbally and with familiar bony elbows against my back, pushing me to toward the wet nose resting on the edge of the bed. I got up, grumbling.

And against my better judgement, I opened the back door, letting in a rush of wet, cool air. And as I had expected, the dog's attention was not on the closest patch of grass but over in the pasture. He disappeared into the darkness at a full run.

By the time I got to the front porch and turned on the floods and grabbed the spotlight, he was across the creek, over in the pasture doing his deer run, back and forth, looking south towards the woods along Nameless Creek. I whistled and hooted, and finally after Ann got up to help me holler over the roar of the frothing creek, the dog's attention turned to coming home.

We had no idea how he could have gotten across the swollen and rising creek the first time, but it was plain to him and to us that getting back was going to be an even bigger problem. The water was still rising fast, and sure enough, the board bridge was gone. Between the dog and the house, the stream was fifteen feet across, several feet deep, frothing, turbulent and powerful as a mining sluice.

We followed Tsuga with the light as he tested the waters and gauged his ability to cross. Both his and our anxiety rose as the rains fell harder and the muddy water roiled angrily. Should I go throw him a rope and hope he'd seen the Lassie episode where she held on with her teeth while her rescuers pulled her to safety? Should I tie myself to a tree and stand midstream and grab the dog by the collar as he came speeding past, a squirming eighty-pound mass of wet-furry flotsam?

Suddenly he disappeared from the spotlight. Where could he be going? He found the widest place, over by the barn where I drive across in the truck. Here, the force of the water was somewhat weaker, but well up his torso. He cut a diagonal path, dog-paddling downstream as the swift current angled him off course. But he made it. From the near bank after a good whole-body shake, the dog ran full tilt back to the house, thoroughly psyched, having had the adventure his wagging tail had warned me of just fifteen minutes earlier.

It took three towels to dry him off. He slept through the night soundly, while I had dreams of inflated barn yard animals bobbing all around me in the muddy waters. A white dog stood on the banks, wagging his tail as I was swept away to sea.

Aging Through the Lens of Time
For the Time, Being

I took no part in time on New Year's Eve, 1950. Events came and marked its passing around me—Christmases and birthdays—measured by the number of fingers I held up, of candles I blew out and made a wish. But time then held no promise, no threat of change in my life. If it moved at all in the order of things, it parted around me, left me untouched. It moved imperceptibly past and was no enemy.

I felt the irresistible pull of time's gravity ten years later. For the first time, I imagined someday, being "old." Up well past my bed time I could see that time was falling, counting down its hours, then the final seconds of 1959. The Big Ball in Times Square fell to earth to welcome a new decade, a number divisible by ten small fingers.

That night I understood with a vague terror that I was at risk for more and more of these decade mileposts ahead in life. I did the math: in the auspicious year of 2000, I would be fifty two. Think of that! In that first moment of comprehension, I looked far ahead into a murky river of time, dreading that I might, after all, be moved along against my will by its current. But maybe not. This unfathomable dimension might pass through me like cosmic rays as I held my place firmly in perpetual youth of heart and mind. And hold my place, I intended to do.

Life beyond eternal childhood held no appeal. I watched with belly rushes as Peter Pan in arched flight soared above the clouds of perpetual youth. I vowed to be a Lost Boy. There at that threshold of the sixties, I tried to imagine aging. I puckered my twelve-year-old face in the mirror, forty years forward, into a wizened distortion of an incomprehensibly-old caricature of myself. I vowed that I would not go peacefully.

And yet, rewards dangled just beyond reach on the infinitely progressing front edge of time—girls, rock and roll, and driving—adventures and delights that growing older dangled in front of me. At fifteen, I was almost ready to put away childish things. Expectations beyond Christmases and birthdays filled a haunting place called The Future. "Wouldn't it be nice if we were older, then we wouldn't have to wait so long" the Beach Boys sang at a high school dance. I felt the pull of tomorrow.

But time by then had become an impediment to the rest of my life, an interminable delay between today and everything I thought I might want in my grown-up life to come. I was stuck in the Terrible Present waiting, year upon plodding year of sub-adulthood to survive. I was held in a sucking bog of frozen youth that, barring a time machine—an understandable and recurrent adolescent fantasy—would have to be traversed if I was to reach the prize: independence, adventure, amour, and freedom from acne. Adulthood.

Ten larger fingers later in 1970—it came so quickly after all— I was married and in graduate school. That year my first camera forever changed how I saw and knew time. Film became a way to preserve present moments in a clear resin of recall. Every photograph set a benchmark in time, held a unique instant in the emulsion of memory, captured in perfect synchrony that vertical line of precise moment that intersects the coordinates of particular place.

No two photographic markers were the same, and there was no going back. With my lens, I fished from the moving stream of time as days flowed through the faces I knew, past the places I loved, leaving the lived, the known moments bobbing on its glassy surface—deeper down, farther back, receding Doppler-like across a realm that I could photograph, could know just once, just now.

I have spent decades more behind the camera, no longer wishing I were older, happy for the past, but savoring photographic instants in the present when one face or one flower, one sunset, yet another family pet or one more grandchild's candle-covered birthday cake fills the viewfinder and moves on downstream.

And when the year 2000 came, lo I was still alive—much to the amazement of the freckled twelve-year-old self I can with such clarity see in the amber of memory, long ago on a New Year's Eve.

My twenty-first century face appeared for real in the mirror that millennial year, no puckering required, pleated by laugh lines and crow's feet, full of wonder, creased like my old first baseman's glove. It was the face of a Lost Boy, riding time like a pair of skates, surfing its glassy surface to the vanishing point, standing still yet moving moment by precious moment through time, aging, after all.

Resolving to Succeed: Our New Year's Hopes
For the Time, Being

Thanksgiving, then Christmas, and now New Years. Since November, you have indulged in late-night conversations and libations with gathered friends and family. You've eaten too much of the wrong things because, heck it's the holidays, so why not? But following on the heels of these excesses and weakly-resisted temptations of the season, it's easy to feel the need to change.

And it's not hard to be sincere about swearing off pastries and staying up late. Your stomach is oh-so-full and you are exhausted from last night's party. Hence, the New Year's Resolution—a tentative resolve to do something different, better, more or less in the coming year than we did in the one just past.

It is a teachable moment, a time of change with potential for the better and not to be taken lightly. There are very few of us that couldn't stand to be better spouses or students, employees, neighbors, or business leaders than we were last year. The clean page of a new calendar ahead offers us all a chance to start our stories afresh.

And so here we are so early in the new year, looking through a window of opportunity ahead when things might be different for us. But if you do what you've always done, you'll get what you've always got. To borrow from Nancy Sinatra, we'll probably keep same-in' when we shoulda been a'changin'. How many January resolutions do you know (your own or others) that have actually been accomplished come the following Christmas?

It's not that we aren't sincere when we declare our fleeting New Year's determination to improve, to grow in new directions or drop one or more of our bad habits. Last week as I took the worn Gary Larsen calendar from the nail on the wall and replaced it with the twelve clean, unblemished pages for the next year, I wondered why January's good intentions so seldom lead to successful accomplishment. Then I realized, at least for me, I had learned part of the answer long ago.

In high school, I was never taught how to plan for success. If it happened, I guess I thought it would be just a happy accident that comes to the few, the privileged. It may be more likely to happen with good grades in school, in knowing the right people, from being at the right place at the right time, from catching a few lucky breaks. But in the end, success—making good goals and achieving them—just happens or not, and I saw myself as a passive sailboat hopeful that favorable winds would come my way, sooner or later. Success would fill my sails. Or it wouldn't.

I was completely disabused of this notion of passive success when I was nineteen. Some forgotten purpose found me in the office of the president of small college where my mother worked as his secretary. On the president's desk were stacks of a small paperback book called Think and Grow Rich by Napoleon Hill. He handed me a copy and encouraged me to read it through at least twice.

"It will change your life" he told me. I am sure I rolled my eyes, at least mentally, anarchic and skeptical product of the sixties as I was. I had no desire to be rich, I remember thinking scornfully. I had seen how miserable my father's most affluent clients were, often because of the anxieties stemming from their wealth. But I did read the book (where I discovered riches could be good things other than money) and the man who gave it to me was right: it changed the way I thought, and thus it has changed my life.

Napoleon Hill, at the request of Andrew Carnegie, interviewed five hundred of the most successful men of the 1930s and found a pattern in their success. Reducing his findings to a phrase, he concluded that "if it can be conceived and believed, it can be achieved." I know that sounds formulaic and simplistic, but applying this book's purposeful approach to life-planning would provide for me a source of focus and structure through a long and checkered history of setting goals for moves to new towns, new jobs and three career changes over the forty years since reading the book. Revisiting clearly-stated goals daily and believing with confidence that they will come to pass really can increase the odds that we will do what we resolve we will do.

I can't help reflecting on this when I put the next year's new calendar on the wall in January—a year in which some stuff will just happen, but during which, too, stuff will happen or not depending on the clarity and force of the goals we set for ourselves today.

So in the end, I guess the point of this little ramble is to wish for you all a new year in which your riches flow from the harvest of the visions of success you create for your future and your neighbor's. I hold a confident hope that acting on the resolutions that grow from those visions will heal, sustain, and bring us to the assurance that next New Years Day, we will have done what's right and best for our families, towns, country and planet.

Never before has the natural world needed each of us to know it, care for it and act on its behalf in such a way as it does in our times. We cannot be responsible stewards of a threatened planet if its creatures are distant, anonymous and irrelevant strangers. Be more aware than you've ever been in this cathedral made without hands, as John Muir called our world. Make friends of its inhabitants—and call them by name.

8

Calling Them by Name
Curious By Nature

On a clear, crisp afternoon in the first week in September, I spotted my first Monarch of the year over a meadow of goldenrod, boneset and milkweed. Twenty of my biology students from Radford University were with me in the field along the New River Trail to see what creatures we might find first hand—and for my students, to give them names for the first time. I held up, pointed out, and identified several dozen flowering plants and trees that afternoon.

Afterwards one young lady asked if we were going to be doing this kind of hands-on outdoor study again. "This is the way I learn best" she said enthusiastically, a fact about herself it seemed she had only that hour discovered.

My students don't see very deeply into nature, it seems, because they've not had much encouragement to look there. So many electronic and virtual distractions compete far too successfully for their attention. They have grown up in an era when our language in the digital world has grown rich while our vocabulary in the real world of nature has become sadly impoverished.

Beyond those kinds of creatures labeled and shrink-wrapped in the grocery store, many of us no longer can call our fellow creatures by name. The naming of things is essential to our understanding of them and to our belonging among them. My students are not sad in the way I am that the hemlocks are dying, because they have never distinguished a hemlock from a tulip poplar. I can't help but think that we'd be better stewards if we knew nature's citizens on a first name basis, and knew more about their families and their kin.

But how can a parent, a teacher or a newly-enlightened field trip student reclaim the names of the things we've forgotten and ignored from the places just beyond our classrooms, shopping malls and speeding cars? Can we learn our way around the meadow or forest where our children are so sadly out of touch? Yes, I think we can, by nurturing intentional vision.

Look for the particulars. Go slowly in nature and stop often. And rekindle curiosity. Learn a dozen trees in summer and fall, and as many wildflowers. Be able to name a ten birds, first by sight, then by their call alone. Identify plants like spicebush, sassafras, and teaberry; scratch and sniff their stems and resurrect the neglected sense of smell that so powerfully builds memories in the out-of-doors. Turn rocks in the stream and learn some salamanders—while they last—and a few dragonflies and even some common spiders and snakes.

Teach your children to see more deeply; then help them find the names for the things they see. This has never been easier to do and you'll be surprised how quickly they learn. The computer is a convenient tool for identification, but my first advice for finding names would be over time to accumulate a small library of field guides that you can carry with you and hold in your hands over the years. Study what you have found while sitting in the grass under the trees and ask for help from your children. Even the smallest can compare pictures.

Never before has the natural world needed each of us to know it, care for it and act on its behalf in such a way as it does in our times. We cannot be responsible stewards of a threatened planet if its creatures are distant, anonymous and irrelevant strangers. Be more aware than you've ever been in this cathedral made without hands, as John Muir called our world. Make friends of its inhabitants— and call them by name.

A Ghost That Lives Off Trees
Earth Companions

It just struck me that this plant looks like Tinkerbell on a stick. (Sorry—just having a HaHa flash of insight!)

But then, having said that, I've given away the answer to my question. How many would have known right away it was a plant? And why might you have paused before saying so? I've had students guess this was a fungus—a mushroom relative. It certainly doesn't look like most of the plants you know. Why?

What you would see right away if this picture were in color is that it is NOT green. So if you learned in school that all plants are green, and this thing isn't green, then by definition it is not a plant. Granted, it's not the usual kind.

It's one of the fairly rare exceptions to our schoolbook rule. There are about 3000 plants that are not green. Beech-drops and squawroot are two more local plants that share this lack of chlorophyll and manage just fine.

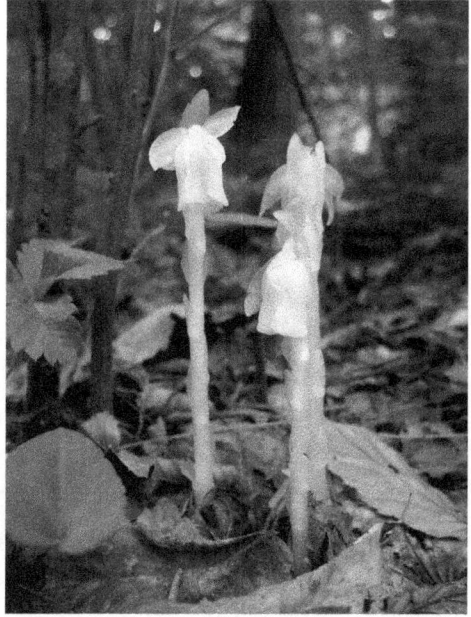

Tinkerbell here is known as Ghost Plant or Indian Pipe, a familiar wildflower of rich woodlands and a member of the blueberry or heath plant family. We find it most often in the deep shade of rhododendrons where not much else can grow for want of enough light to power photosynthesis.

But if this is a plant but it doesn't make its own food, don't you wonder how it survives? I was prepared to tell you that it was a parasite off of the nutrients in tree roots, but I just learned (in one of those fun AHA moments!) that this is not entirely true. Ghost Plant connects by way of a middleman, a special kind of fungus, to get its food from a host tree.

So enters the mushroom group into the story after all—in the form of masses of microscopic threads called mycorhizae—literally "fungus roots." We know now that some 80-90% of land plants (including many crop species and grains) depend on this mutualistic feeding relationship in the soil to thrive. The fungus gets sugars from the plant, the plant gets nutrients from soil it couldn't get on its own.

Alone, neither would do very well. We know far less than we need to know—about mycorhizae, about earthworms, about topsoil replacement—if we are to take adequate care of the precious earth in agricultural soils, timbered woodlands, tree farms and rain forests. Once lost, can a healthy soil be restored?

A Handful of Spiders
Earth Companions

You may have heard the odd didgeridoo sound outdoors at some time, even if you've never bothered to look for the insect that was making it. Next time you have the chance, follow the droning high-pitched whine and look high on the walls under the eaves of a house, barn or tool shed. Ah ha! There it is! You've found the source of the racket and it is coming from inside some odd clay-pipe-looking thing plastered to the wall in the shade of the roof. You have found the nursery of a solitary wasp—the mud or dirt dauber sometimes called the Organ Pipe Wasp.

Watch the nest for a while, and you'll see the adult female wasp emerge and disappear. (The male usually stands guard somewhere nearby.) If you're able to keep up with her flight, you will see the wire-waisted blue-black female searching wet soil of your yard for the right kind of mud. Be patient and you'll see her carry away a ball of it to add to the cylindrical tube of the nest. Once the tube is the right length, she begins to bring home the baby food: an assortment of spiders from nearby.

When she finds a spider, she stings and sedates it and places it in the interior of the tube. When enough spiders fill the tube, she lays an egg there and seals it closed. Mind you, the spider-food is drugged, not killed. The spiders (like the orb weavers you see here) will remain alive but paralyzed until the wasp egg hatches to a larva and begins to eat its way through its stored food.

Serving suggestion: take a putty knife or other blunt blade and dislodge one or two tubes from the wall. Catch the nest debris and uneaten spiders in a pan. If you find a hole at the base of a tube that means the matured wasp that was inside has eaten all the spiders and made its escape into the world to get a job, have a family, and start making house payments.

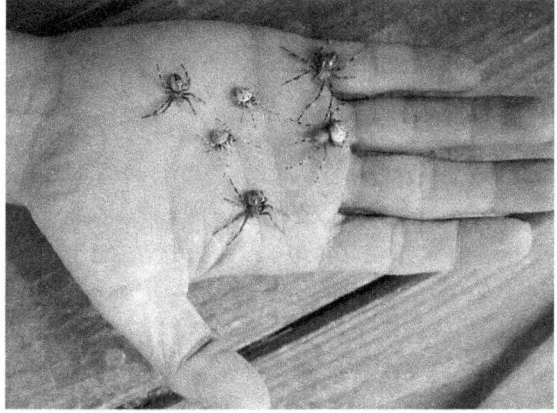

The spiders (sorry you can't see the cyan, light green, pale orange and yellow colors here within individuals of this single species) are limp but alive. They may even move around a little in their comas, but they can't hurt you. Are you brave enough to hold some of them in your hand? It took some convincing to get my son here to do it.

So now, next time you hear the whirring from the wall, you'll know all about who is making the sound and why, and even be willing to hold a dozen spiders in the palm of your hand! Or maybe not.

Making Other Arrangements
Within Our Means

With all the strength I could muster, I helped a man push his stalled car across the gentle grade of a parking lot last week. There were three of us there, heaving, leaning into the ton of metal on wheels. We moved the car less than fifty feet in the end, and when we were done, even the youngest of us was winded and shaky.

That hard work of human muscle power came to mind a few days later, when, without so much as a thought, I throttled up the speed of the Subaru—40, 50, 60 miles an hour—up the pitch of the quarter mile ramp from Dixie Caverns to merge with 70 mph tractor-trailers on the interstate.

If I and my car had to be moved (at any speed) by people power up the length of this incline, how many more men like me (heck, even the lean and wiry me of 30 years ago) would it have taken to accomplish this same force over distance?

It was as if I had harnessed in my car's engine the power of energy slaves that were taking the place of human force, my puny performance in the parking lot still remembered.

In my mind's eye on that highway ramp appeared a long line of muscular, loin-clothed workers. Thirty up front pulled hard on ropes attached to my bumper, another twenty behind were pushing, struggling, and I—some kind of aristocratic nobility at his ease—sat comfortably inside with the windows rolled up, listening to Credence Clearwater Revival while fifty powerful hydrocarbon slaves did the heavy lifting.

We humans do so little real physical work anymore because, for the last century and a half, we've had these marvelous energy slaves whose muscle so enormously exceeds our own. And we have taken our ease, reliant on an ever-flowing tap of Texas Tea.

We have understood the many advantages of condensed liquid energy from the first of the fossil fuel era, comparing work done by our coal and gas powered machines in terms of the work that had been done by our first and since abandoned energy slaves other than fire and our fellow man: horses. Horse power.

They were fine while they lasted, horses and oxen and such, but they were messy, required lots of space and feed and were subject to injury and disease. So when we could put the power of many horses and man-years of labor in a barrel on a ship or truck, and from there into an engine on a farm, why would civilization not be ecstatic! Horsepower without the horse!

Consider this (from Thomas Dixon's The Upside of Down): "Three large spoonfuls of crude oil contain about the same amount of energy as eight hours of human manual labor. When we fill our car with gas, we're pouring into the tank the energy equivalent of about two years of human manual labor."

If the twenty gallons in my tank equals two years of human effort, a 42 gallon barrel of refined petroleum is about four years worth of people power. The

US uses 21 million barrels a day (2008). Do the math. See the pyramids our slaves have built us over the years.

It is on that energy-dense, super-portable, abundant and everyman-affordable commodity that our modern civilization has been built. But all that, by the reckoning of a growing number of observers and historians of energy, is about to change. And we need to be making other arrangements.

We don't know exactly when, how or how fast global civilization will of necessity transition into a post-peak restructuring (oh the magnitude of cultural change loaded in that innocuous word) but come it will. And it will come as no surprise to some.

A certain Mr. Hubbert projected in 1956 (with alarming accuracy, it turns out) that the discovery and extraction of oil would follow a bell-shaped curve. There would be a top of the curve representing the maximum productivity (reached for US oil production in 1970) and on the other side of the crest of that curve of global production (not a few argue we are there), while there would still remain some years-worth of oil in the ground, production would decline along pretty much the same slope as it had been discovered and used.

Problem is, since demand has always kept pace with the volume of oil that can be produced, while the production curve heads down, the demand upslope continues to rise. It ascends along the unaltered path of our long history of addiction and dependence and is compounded by the needs of rising populations that are new to the oil economy—China and India and Indonesia—who want dominion over the number of energy slaves the average American has "owned" for many decades in our first-world economy.

At some point—when it takes a barrel of oil to produce a barrel of oil—and energy investment is the same as energy return, the end of our short history of oil energy slavery will have arrived.

That will change everything. And we must be proactive enough to plan ahead of need for how that will impact food production, work commutes and the kinds of jobs people do, education, housing and city planning, health care, manufacturing, entertainment—not a single segment of human enterprise will be untouched.

As this change comes upon us, we may be resilient. Or we may be brittle. What should a town and county like ours or yours be doing—now? We have incredible resources in the skills and knowledge of those who live among us. I for one would be gratified to see the conversations begin in earnest.

Wellness and the Power of Hope
Not Fish Nor Fowl

Well how about that—I can wear sandals again this summer! Let me explain.

I wasn't all that faithful to follow the home remedy my physician friend described to me this time last year. He said it would take several months to work. It took twelve. But putting Vicks VapoRub on my big toenail—whenever I happened to remember to do it—has finally defeated the invasive microbe that had blemished my otherwise perfect tootsies!

The treatment of choice for this condition from a pharmaceutical point of view is a bona fide medicine—very expensive, very liver-toxic, and not one I was willing to ingest for the four to six months it required. But millions of dollars were spent perfecting its formulation to do exactly what I needed it to do. Shouldn't I have gone with the real deal?

Was it even possible in the end that a cheap over-the-counter ointment could have had any therapeutic impact whatsoever on such an off-label foot condition? I wondered.

Maybe my body chemistry rallied an attack against this fungal invader because—based on the authoritative word of the doctor—I simply expected to get better. Every time I applied the menthol-scented goo, I imagined little fungal filaments under my toenail writhing in agony.

I watched for and expected signs of retreat. But in the end, it might have been nothing but the placebo effect that gave me back my summer sandals. Would mayonnaise or toothpaste applied with great expectations have worked just as well? (I once had a patient who confessed that he believed there might actually be something to the Gazebo Effect. But that's another story.)

But wait: "nothing but...?" Perhaps we've been too dismissive, too hasty in our modern western scientific sophistication to pretend the effect of a placebo is no more than a medical embarrassment.

Merck hates it when we consider it, but in many cases the curative potential of our own expectations and hopes of wholeness seem to be as big a part of our recovery from illness as the expensive purple pills picked up as we pass quickly through the pharmacy drive-in window.

The Latin term "placebo" literally translates "I will please." Too often, the word has carried only that sense of a counterfeit substance or of a dishonest act employed more to please the patient than to make them well. But study after study shows that sugar pills and saline injections and other sham treatments truly exert a healing influence on our minds and bodies often equal to or even exceeding the "real" treatment.

Those subjects who thought they got the real knee surgery (but only got the scalpel punctures) walk afterward with a reduction of post-op pain as great as those who had the real arthroscopy procedure. Those who believed they got fetal stem cells implanted in their brains have their Parkinson's symptoms improve just like the subjects who really did get the implants. The clinically depressed people who got sugar pills show the same brain PET-scan changes as those who received the scientifically-validated medicine and improved.

I have nothing to back this up, but I'm guessing that the reverse is probably also true. If we feel our health care plans are unfair or providers are not listening; if those who should care for us seem always to be too busy to come fully into the whole of our lives; if we are treated only through chemical means about which the physician or pharmacist seems ambivalent—then are we not less likely to benefit from whatever internal mechanism could be at work in our belief system inherent in the placebo effect?

As faith erodes in the medicine-as-business quest for efficiency, productivity and the continued good health of the corporation, what sum total of possible healing has gone unrealized?

As a therapist once burned out on insurance-driven health care, I think about this a lot. When I see my physical therapy patients in the clinic, I am thankful for the one-on-one treatment sessions where the time I spend hearing their stories and the touch of a caregiver's hand heals them, I am convinced, as much as the ultrasound I apply or exercises I ask them to do.

When they feel they have been heard and cared for, they begin listening to a different internal script about their future well-being. They begin to hand over their condition—with a name now and a proposed solution—to me. A hopeful and trusting patient with a supportive caregiver is far more likely to improve.

The jury is still out on just how the power of suggestion brings about healing just as it is undetermined how and when and if placebos should be made a regular part of medical practice. But it seems certain our overall health is more likely to improve as we regain our trust in those who treat us well.

And next time you go, thank your doctor for spending time with you. And ask him if he thinks Vicks VapoRub might be just the thing for whatever it is that ails you.

Moon Shadows

Blue razor shadows tangle
bare bones of trees
against the shoulders of hills
white daggers
angled from behind
dark translucence buried
in new snow

Eyes exposed to silver bright,
make seamless memory
from sigh of wind, smell of cold
And then, a motion,
somewhere, movement—

Like the flicker of a silent movie
and again. Not movement sudden
faintly at the edge of vision
subtle, massive and unnamed.

With lunacy and light
the valley fills, empties as
dark waves surge past,
and another—
an armada—cloudships
propelled by moonbeams.

White light and blue, they came
in liquid shadows shades of gray
the size of meadows Surging
from behind us—under our feet
poured into creeks and quickly away
rising without effort under
snow under oaks
to the top of the ridge and gone.

And the world flashed
from life to death
from shadow of cloud to
light of the Unfamiliar
and I am terrified and I
am made whole—
a frail vapor so close to heaven
so In love with this pulsing world.

Our Fortress Garden Worth the Costs
Body and Soul Together

I stand half-hopeful in this rectangle of lawn whose lines bound our renewed attempt at vegetable gardening. A window of sky, a patch of earth and the economy of nature: how perfect it will be. The heart soars.

And then it crashes back to the cold damp earth again. All of nature has worked against the possibility of our having a successful vegetable garden, I remember painfully, still feeling the sting of last year's total failure to feed ourselves.

In this water-gouged crease of northeastern Floyd County, our day-lit hours are not as long nor our soils as soon warmed as garden plots west of us and higher up. And more than that, the blessed solitude and freedom from traffic we enjoy in this isolated frost pocket translates to a very safe haven indeed for far too many deer. Rats-on-Stilts, we call them.

And so, for the past few years, I have darkly referred to our beleaguered, would-be garden as The Wildlife Salad Park. Scarecrows, pie-pans on strings, hair and other human sprinklings have failed to discourage the deer from jumping the electric fence and helping themselves. But this year, we're upping the ante.

Stopping short of razor wire, the new containment even so will look from the road like a concentration camp for cabbage and carrots. And if deer can jump an eight foot fence of cattle panels, well they'll soon be turning door knobs and coming inside to raid the fridge. At that point, I'll say uncle.

This new garden space is closer to the house—not that these deer give a rip about proximity of humans or their meager pets. The newly-turned plot in contrast to the old one will get another couple of hours more sun and is not over the septic field. And surely the stalag fence will help keep out the deer—if not the crows, moles, grubs, wilts and rots with which gardeners also compete for those coveted Mason jars of green and gold.

We'll be hoping this time next year to be planting seeds saved from this year's non-hybrid varieties—many of which lack the perfect shapes and brightest colors or blight resistance of the Big Seed Company hybrids. By saving seeds, we hold on to a little more control of where our food comes from. We'd best be thinking a lot more about that.

We'll be thankful for adequate and well-timed rains this summer, and failing that, for enough flow in the creek to water rows with buckets. Goose Creek vanished completely in the drought of 2003, so mulching to keep in the ground what moisture we get is one of our goals.

Our Fortress Garden will have its costs, it's true. (I figure by the time we're 206, we'll have paid for our free vegetables.) But we think of the greater costs of being dependent on unsustainable agri-industry to ship to us what we can grow locally for ourselves. We consider how good it tastes to eat sugar peas fresh from the vine.

To have a garden again will enlighten, entertain and reconnect us to the geology, geography, climate and biology of where we live. And by golly, we'll put our garden behind a stockade wall if we must before we'll let the deer take that away from us.

Whither Winter Weather?
Within These Walls

If the TV Weather Persons are right about the coming winter—and the Woolly Bears are wrong—I predict that it will be cold and wet. Or not. From either meteorological source, your mileage may vary.

It IS the weather after all. But it seems that for the winter of 2008-9, for what it's worth, the consensus of opinion is that it will be "colder and wetter" than usual for much of the eastern US.

The first predictions that Floyd County was in for a doozy of a winter came in response to the productive and abundant summer we just had. I'd never heard that one before, but it makes sense.

"Oh yeah" said one local old-timer, "if we have a bumper crop of walnuts, the gardens are full of produce and apple trees hanging heavy, why, that's nature's way of providing for the wild creatures in the hard winter we'll be having." (Paradoxically, there are NO acorns over most of Virginia this year.)

That prospect seems thoughtfully efficient on the part of natural providence, merciful at the hand of a caring god whose eye is on the sparrow (if not the squirrels of '08) and poetic to the romantics among us. But is it accurate and should we lay up more of those potatoes, apples and beans than we would ordinarily keep in the root cellar to see us through the hard, cold and snowy months to come?

Of course we would not be good rural mountain folk if we did not consider in our prognostication what the Woolly Bear caterpillars tell us is coming our way. I could never keep straight their supposed black versus brown message.

Consequently, my rule of the Woolly Bear has always been that, when I see them in great urgency crossing the roads seeking shelter in October (and to my wife's horror swerve to miss them), no matter what the mix of brown to black, it will be more or less cold sooner or later and I'll need a furry coat like theirs to keep me warm.

Since ignorance is bliss, I'll pretend not to read the evidence that, if there is a weather-predicting shift at all in fur color of a year's population of Woolly Worms, they get it right about half the time. Weather prophet? Not exactly. Toss a quarter, you call it. So where can we turn for winter wisdom? A hundred years ago, how'd a farmer figure how much hay he'd need for the winter ahead?

To predict tomorrow's weather, look at today's. The Amish say, "August fog blooms winter's snow." Wow. That means folks over on perpetually-fogbound Walnut Knob near the Blue Ridge Parkway are in for it, while we here on Goose Creek, not so much.

Another measure of winter to come is said to be the frequency with which yellow jackets build nests in the ground. Yikes. Keep a VDOT snow plow at the top of Shawsville Pike because we're going to get buried down here this winter!

Joe Bastardi, chief long-range forecaster for AccuWeather, is calling for one of the coldest, snowiest winters in years in the East (that's just barely north of us) that will be one to tell your grandchildren about. Following an active hurricane summer and with currently cooler South Pacific and Gulf waters, some places will surely see a colder, wetter winter this year. Or not.

In the end, we will augur the future months' weather from all the signs at our disposal and take our chances. Whimsy or wisdom, brain or heart? Wet finger in the wind or the home anemometer dial on your desk? Your guess is as good as any.

We'll hope for the best and prepare for the worst. Hunker down, neighbors. Keep the snow shovel handy just in case. Have plenty of cocoa on hand, bring in an extra cat and toss another log on the fire.

Because three black crows called on a cloudless day from the roof of our barn in October, I predict a more or less pleasant third month of the year by and by if we can just hang on through the hard or not-so-hard winter of '08.

The Greatest Gift: Our Stories
For the Time, Being

From my window seat I looked down on cobalt blue cloud shadows drifting slowly east across great green patches of forest. Their shapes shifted like Rorschach blots against the landscape and my mind conjured meaning and memories in their patterns. I was going home, back to Birmingham where so many of the parts of my life took root and form, going home for Mothers Day, the first with her since 2001.

That was the year when my mother, my wife and I had been traveling and away on Mothers Day. As we walked up the ramp into the Charlotte terminal on our return trip, we were startled to hear our names announced on the loud speakers. At the information desk, we learned the sad news that my mother's mother had died in the nursing home during the week we were gone. My grandmother's stories that I never knew were perhaps that day's greatest tragedy, and I was thinking about those conversations that she and I never had as I walked to my gate at the Charlotte airport on my recent visit south to see my mother, almost exactly five years later.

Mom is eighty now, independent and vigorous, and she still drives—very, very slowly. She picked me up at the Birmingham airport and for a couple of hours, we revisited every place on the south side of town she thought I might remember. Each suburban street held stories of neighbors good or bad, of the local pets we both remembered by name, of girlfriends—names forgotten. Mom learned of petty pranks and transgressions of youth only now confessed. We pieced together the story of our lives from the places where they had happened. This was the same, that had changed.

"I may have told you this" she would begin, and without hesitating for a response, proceed to retell her mother's perspective about episodes in my young life from her adult point of view back in another age. I had heard most of it before. I so wanted to hear it again, because these connections with who and where we once had been are all too easy to forget with the geography that separates us now.

Back home at her apartment on Mother's Day 2006, I discovered that over the years, she had been recording her life story, putting down details remembered about her mother, and about her own childhood in Birmingham, a home town that she never left; about a grandfather that I never met, who died in a hunting accident when she was eleven; about her boyfriends and the sad-romantic times of the war years.

She and I listened to the tape together, recorded haltingly in her sweet southern voice, little changed from those scratchy records from her public speaking classes at Woodlawn High School in the early '40s. She was passing on her stories to her children and family in her own voice, so that we would not forget.

Funny how things work out. I had come to see my mother on Mothers Day with a gift: the book I had written as a bridge between us. There wouldn't be so many meetings ahead for the two of us now, and my hope had been to finish Slow Road Home while she was here to know of it, to share with me in the accomplishment of this personal milestone, to hold my stories in her hand.

And in return, she placed in my hands her tape—a mutual transfusion of family story from her life and era into my own. On Mothers Day, 2006, we gave these gifts to each other while there was yet time. And I hoped that somewhere, my grandmother was watching.

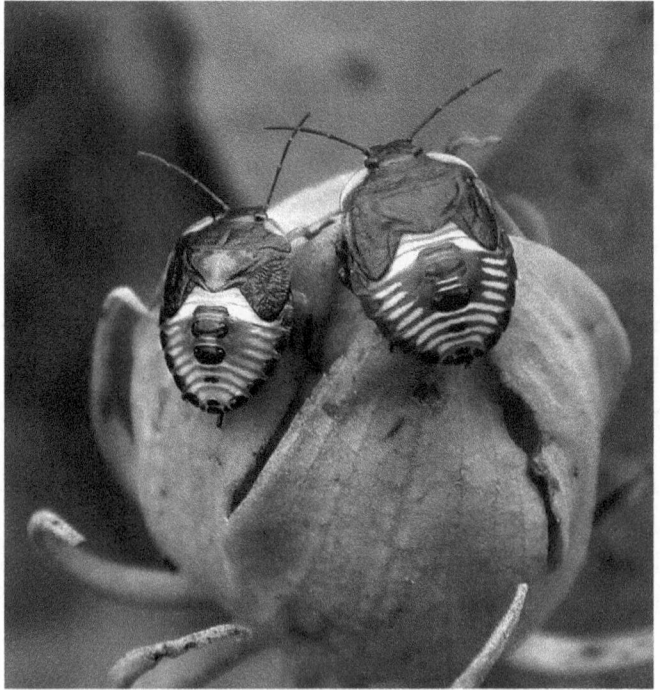

There is a creeping ambivalence in our relationship each year with the chain saw, splitting maul and black plastic in the wind. Staying warm some future winter may be a matter of turning up a dial. Perhaps the heat pump cometh, but not today, not this year when we have enough in the stacks to see us through 'til April. We have our health, mostly, and we have Advil. And there will likely be windfalls yet to come.

9

The Ah, the A-ha and The Ha-Ha
Curious By Nature

You can't buy these Gifts from nature, but trust me—all three will be granted if you expect to receive them. You'll probably remember having known them as a child, maybe even later—for a while. With a little reminding here you can learn to find and treasure them again in an intentional "green hour" as a grown-up.

Mind you, this is just my way of thinking about the wisdom and pleasure that I find in the natural world. These little exclamations I'm telling you about also apply in the discovery of science, the satisfaction of the beautiful and in the energy of creative wit and humor.

The three short and similar-sounding terms that I have in mind are: Aha. Ah. And Haha. (I first read about the role of these concepts long ago in Arthur Koeslter's Act of Creation, later paraphrased by someone else with these short words; I did not invent this usage except to apply it to our relationship with nature.)

The Aha! is a moment of meaningful personal discovery. Ah comes from a deep and soul-satisfying appreciation of beauty or harmony. And Haha is that flash of humorous revelation when two realms collide in a new and startling way. Let's briefly take a look at each of these deeply-meaningful terms from personal experience so you'll recognize them "in the field."

Aha! springs from what we see, hear, touch, taste and smell. And if you learn to go slowly, stop often and expect a small discovery from every outing, you'll be rewarded, rarely returning home without at least one Aha. For me, every photograph records a unique moment in place, a one-of-a-kind experience—a discovery of light, shape, texture or form. Science begins with Aha experiences—measured, recorded, and most often seen with the eyes. Curiosity is its driving energy.

While seeing, don't neglect the other senses. Discover sounds too faint for those who hurry past—insects under the bark of the tree you lean against; the drip-drip of sap from tree branches on the first warm days of March. Hear the difference in the shush of wind through bare branches in winter and the leafy wind of spring in the same woods.

Scratch and sniff for Aha moments of the nose. Learn the smell of where you live. Teaberry plants and sweet birch twigs smell like chewing gum! Common Liverworts smell like "wax lips" and some millipedes gently shaken smell like cherries. Don't miss the discoveries your nose can give you. The memories that outdoor fragrances offer can last a lifetime.

The satisfied Ah is more internal and personal. You might think of it as your response to the art of nature realized in those wonderful moments when you are smitten by the rightness and goodness of the world at hand. Ah is your response to beauty and truth. It is the way you digest in a deeper part of your soul the Aha facts, understanding them in some small way that shows with satisfaction or awe your own unique part in the cosmos.

Ah is the sound of your enjoyment of the music of nature, of its rhythm and cadence; its nuances of light and shadow, piano and forte, tragedy and comedy, tenor, bass and harmony. Ah is the touching of the Other in forest or meadow, mountaintop or beach and in ourselves. It often finds its end in thankfulness and joy. Awe is a close cousin of Ah.

Haha the release that comes when you suddenly make sense of separate and at first seemingly-unrelated facts. All at once, two frames of reference merge and you get the joke. We are shocked, shaken, and pleased at a new way of seeing things. The punch line comes. We laugh, tension released.

Outdoors, we see (or can learn once again to see) in billowing summer clouds that a toad is eating a giraffe! We come home with a photograph of a wild hibiscus with a pair of immature stinkbugs on it and realize suddenly that it is a face with two wide-staring eyes under heavy eyebrows, sporting a smirking grin and an attitude! The world is full of metaphors—this is like that! These unexpected connections bring us humor and joy and a new way of seeing. The Haha in nature is close cousin to whimsy and delight. It thrives on imagination!

The Three Gifts found in the outdoors nearby—the Aha, the Ah and the Haha—are the muses that would lead us to wonder. And in wonder is the beginning of wisdom.

Mystery, Myth and Matters of Fact
Earth Companions

Inside the rustic cabin a few easy miles from the heart of Camp Winnataska, a dozen ten year old campers scrambled to choose bunks, exhausted from the longest hike some of these Birmingham city boys had ever taken in their short lives.

The chatter waned toward a whisper as night fell. "What if there are bears and stuff out there!" wondered one of our charges, a wonderfully terrible idea that quickly morphed into an hour of swapping lies, ghost stories and legends of woodland monsters.

As the tall tales finally began to wear down somewhat towards bedtime, another camp leader and I slipped away. We could still hear the buzz of conversation inside through the thin walls. In the near-dark we hauled a campfire stump over next to the cabin so I could reach the corrugated metal roof with a claw-like branch. Scratch scratch with the branch on the metal; we waited.

"Listen!" a high-pitched voice broke through the background chatter followed by collective holding of the breath. "Did you hear that?" Scratch. Wait.

And when the timing was just right, I let loose my "mountain lion" scream through cupped hands—a growling, throat-rending scream modeled after the terrible howl of man-eating tigers on Tarzan. But for our purposes that dark and starry night, this was the terrible cry of a Mountain Lion. We'd planted that seed earlier during the forest monster stories.

"Why yes, we lost a camper up here coupla years back" we'd told them. "Started off hiking towards this cabin with thirteen kids your age and when we got here, there were only twelve. Found most of little Kenny back along the trail we walked today, draped across a fork of a big oak, about ten feet up—where she pulled him for dinner. Man!"

We half believed it ourselves, so common were the tales we'd heard from our seniors, obliged as each generation is to pass on to the next the fear and reverence we owe to the legend of the Big Cats.

I bring this up because twice, in totally independent party conversations over the recent holidays, I heard grown men in tight little knots of conversation, perpetuating myth and rumor, tales of encounters and sworn testimony of reputable folk declaring the Certain Truth of these ultimate predators among us.

The believers swear that they (or more often someone they know who knows someone who) got a good look at the tail—almost as long as the body. "Now don't tell me that was a tabby or a bob cat, no sir. And I was (or the other guy was) sober as a judge" they swear.

If a big cat was to want to be left to himself, he could hardly find a better place than our remote end of Floyd County. Yes, I can imagine Mountain Lions out there, padding along in the moon shadows silently up on our ridge tonight.

Those majestic predators were once common across all of Virginia and North America. Their demise in the East was in part because of the dwindling of the deer population. Well that particular item is prominently back on the menu, with only the local pack of Killer Subarus to keep deer numbers in check. Unless...

Rumors abound. We want to believe. But I am, at times, a rational man, a science-oriented kind of guy not given to Elvis sightings. And so, in light of the recent party conversations and the pervasive hope and conviction there are "painters" in our woods, I did some studying on the matter of the Cougar of Floyd County and the East.

Here are the facts in a nutshell: a couple of organizations (like easterncougar.org) exist with the chief purpose of investigating purported records of eastern cougars. I want to believe, but listen: "Since the ECF's inception in 1998, years of fielding, following up, and soliciting evidence from such reports have failed to produce a single cougar confirmation." Oh ye of little faith.

If they are in fact not here (and I know some folks, sober as judges, who swear they've seen them) they ought to be—on Wills Ridge, in Free State and along the Little River. We gain by that hope and belief that wildness lives immortal just beyond our door.

And these magnificent reminders of life's fine balance do live as we sustain their existence in our imaginations—generation after generation of campers, hunters, tellers of tales—believing we might reach the crest one day and see a panther disappearing into the distance.

We imagine them out there, watching, even as you read this final sentence, watching without a sound; waiting. Scratch scratch.

Sea Change May Alter the Tide of History
Within Our Means

"If you do what you've always done, you'll get what you've always got" says the old bromide. I have to remind myself of this folksy phrase when I find myself stuck in the deep ruts of habit, going 'round the same fruitless loops over and over again. If the ingredients each time are the same, so will be the soup. So if you want different flavors and textures, you'll have to put different ingredients into the blender.

Doing things differently is both blessing and curse. We go on vacation for the joy and excitement of doing things differently. We watch fiction movies and read novels to see and imagine something other than the routine realities of our ordinary lives. But for the most part if we're honest, we abhor change in the real world and cherish the fixed and comfortable routine in the way we approach our days at work or home and in our relationships. First the pants, then the shoes. Cereal in the same bowl, coffee in the same cup. News at six.

We structure our thinking about the world on a foundation of assumptions about How Things Are. We build our realities, values, expectations and beliefs on top of those foundations year after year and understandably, we resist the threat of change that would require us to renovate. The deeper those changes need to go toward the basement to replace the termite-infested wrong assumptions, the more change unsettles us and the more resistant we become to disturbing the status quo.

I pull at this tangled thread of thought here in an election year at the end of a long game of partisan badminton that batted back and forth the word CHANGE that both parties competed ad nauseam to get into their platforms, their pitches and their robocalls. Chances are, we are all pretty sick of the word by now.

But we don't have the luxury to sit on our laurels or other body parts and think the changes that lie ahead can be left to the next administration. I don't have the answers for how to pull this off, but I'm starting to comprehend the full impact of the questions and would love some company in discussing just what lies ahead for all of us—and especially for our children.

There are changes and there are changes. The one kind we're used to would simply move the same pieces around in a different order—add the celery first instead of third—or toss in a dash more salt. That's yesterday's recipe for change. The second and far more foundation-rattling kind of change that looms ahead of us today is sometimes referred to as "sea change."

From Shakespeare's Tempest we've adopted the phrase to mean a profound transformation—a complete shift in our world view and way of thinking. Sea change is a kind of metamorphosis, a caterpillar goes in and a butterfly comes out.

What is called for if we are to successfully face the problems and predicaments of the future is this kind of change. (I heard it said recently that problems are matters we solve, predicaments are matters we deal with. We have plenty of both.)

Our personal, national and planetary well-being are at risk in ways and to degrees that human civilization has never known. How so many billions of us will eat and drink, heat and cool, travel, build and prosper in an enfeebled and moribund future world seem insoluble conundrums given our old way of dealing with them.

So then, why am I hopeful? Because for the first time in decades—and maybe to a degree never seen before—even politicians are beginning to grapple with the notion that we can't count on the old kind of change to sustain our future. They are remembering the inconvenient truth that economies are at root built on the soil. Many world leaders now acknowledge that humans must think and act with greater respect toward all races and the biology of the planet if we are to survive as state, nation and species.

I'm encouraged that young people are once again becoming actively engaged in the fate of their future. I am heartened that a world of voices amplified and compounded by the Internet are speaking out in favor of bottom-up community-based solutions to many of these problems. Even Americans are starting to think in terms of the little they need out of the sum of what they have come to desire.

To reach the distant shore of an uncertain future, we can't just do what we've always done. As this wave of change comes to our here and now, we can float like flotsam or sink like a stone; but if we make the choice to do so, we can paddle for all we're worth and the flow of change will transform us for a future fit for living.

Child Evangelism
Not Fish Nor Fowl

This odd piece is obviously different from the rest of the pieces here, written in a rare writers' workshop. It's fun to read before audiences using my native Alabama schoolboy delivery—a diction and twang since appropriated by Forest Gump.

I like my accordion. It's new and smells like new shoes. My momma let me get the one with blue sparkles in the sharps and flats when I was ten years old. And when they hear me playing it out on the sidewalk and come around, the kids from the project always want mostly to push on the sparkly keys. I pull the bellows back and forth to make some air come out, cause if I don't they wont be able to hear the notes.

I don't like it that their hands are dirty. My momma makes me come here. On Thursdays we pick up Miss Sharp. She comes with us and she smells like a room full of roses. Our car smells like her on Friday. She dudn't have a car or any kids. When I play and the kids come, it's like they belong to her. She seems happy to be there.

While Miss Sharp sets up the easel, momma says to me "Play Way Down Upon the Suwanee River." It's really hot and the accordion makes me sweat and itch. When the kids come, it's dusty 'cause they wore off all the grass. I don't want to play loud cause I feel silly; but momma tells me "Play louder!"

The first time, not many of them came. Now, they know 'bout us. I put down a jelly samwich one time and watched the big black ants come get it. When I play "Pop Goes the Weasel" the kids come from all around and I think they look like ants. First they bunch up and mash the keys on my accordion. Then they sit down in a circle, except it's not a jelly sandwich they come for. It's Miss Sharp. She's nice to them and tells stories.

This iddn't a nice place. Momma says the people who live here are 'less fortunate than ourselves'. That means they fight a lot and make noise in their houses, all in lots of long buildings that have fans in the windows. There is broken glass and we have to be careful. I have shoes but some of the kids who come got no shoes. After I'm done playin', we get in a sort of circle and sing "If you're happy and you know it" and sometimes "There's within my heart a melody." Miss Sharp's throat goes up and down when she sings and she throws her head way back like a rooster crowin'. Momma says we shouldn't be ashamed of our faith. Miss Sharp iddn't ashamed. She's in Child Evangelism.

I get to play with the flannel pieces in the back seat when momma drives us over to Elyton Village. One time Miss Sharp brought David and Goliath. It sure took a big piece of flannel to make Goliath. There are some other people in the story made of flannel, soft and bright, but I don't know who they are. And there is a sword. And David's sling.

I didn't rightly know what a sling was. When we were sitting in the dust in a circle in the sun with the broken glass and the fans going in the windows and the people inside yelling and the crickets making noise and Miss Sharp smiling and talking to us kids, I listened to the part in the story about the sling. She said it was made of string and a pouch thing. You can throw a rock hard and kill a giant with a sling, she told us. I like throwing rocks.

When we're done with the story, we sing "The B I B L E, yes that's the book for me." We take Miss Sharp and her flannel board home. And it smells nice in the car. I am real glad to get home. We have grass and it's quiet there.

When I got home one day from the projects, I wanted to make me a sling to throw rocks. I got me some string from the kitchen drawer and a blue jeans patch from the round tin of sewing stuff in the hall closet. I made me a sling. It looked like the little piece of flannel in the story. I didn't know how to make it work. I couldn't wait to ask my Sunday School teacher and he told me how. I went home and spun a rock round and round and let go! But it didn't go where I wanted, it went backwards and hit the house. My momma came outside to see what happened, and she saw my sling. She said "Where did you get that!" and I told her Miss Sharp told me how to make it and Mr. Eisel my Sunday School teacher told me how to use it. She said the devil had got hold of my ears and I should hear the Christian parts of the stories.

When us kids went back to school in the fall, we stopped going to the projects. I was glad 'cause I was running out of songs to play. And it didn't look like Miss Sharp was gonna tell us about any other neat smoting stories about spears and slings and stuff.

A few years later, I made a sling out of leather. I could make a rock go where I wanted, twice as far as the other boys could throw without a sling. Pretty soon the colored boys was making slings too. And me and some boys that lived on my block had rock fights with the nigra boys on the power company land that summer. It was 1963 and the growed-up white folk and the colored in Birmingham were unhappy with each other about something. But us kids, we were just having a friendly rock fight using our slings, just like the one in the flannel board stories.

You know, I think Miss Sharp'd be happy if she knew how much I'd learned from her that summer. But Momma says I prob'bly shouldn't say nothing to Miss Sharp about all that.

Your World and Mine: From a Distance
Local Color

I've been flying all over the planet these past months, soaring from the equator to the poles. I travel to new places, looking down tens or hundreds of miles from my earth orbiting spacecraft or upper-atmospheric spy plane; or I hover for a closer look at ten thousand feet in my hot-air balloon. My craft is called Google Earth, and it is not a toy.

For a map-loving arm-chair explorer like me, this free digital globe program is the most wonderful educational tool to come along in my not-particularly-well traveled life! I've followed the waters of the Nile and the New Rivers from their sources to their respective oceans. I've found the highest peaks of all the great mountain ranges from the Andes to the Appalachians. I've soared over Pakistan, Madagascar, Chile, New Zealand and Afghanistan and learned things about each place that I never would have grasped from a textbook description or from a flat black and white picture of these places.

I am mystified as the world turns below with a slight nudge of the computer mouse. It stands against the blackness of space, a seamless and unified blue marble that has been compared to a single, large living cell.

No artificial lines divide the Koreas, no boundaries show between the Hindu nation and the Muslim nation next door; they are all of one piece. Northern Ireland blends imperceptibly with the south. There is no color coding to divide the red states from the blue.

From a Space Station view, it looks as if there should be plenty of room, adequate air and soil, and enough of every necessity for all the humans, plants and animals invisible below who live together on the Water Planet. From a distance, it seems such a pleasant Eden, but going down for a closer look sometimes bursts my bubble of perfect-world fantasy.

On my first high-altitude visit over the Amazon rain forests of Brazil, an odd smudge caught my attention, even from five hundred miles up. A bottle-brush pattern of lighter strokes stood out against the darkest green of untouched forest. A double-click on the spot took me down, down for a closer view to satisfy my curiosity. Below me, from a main road 200 miles long, ten-mile side roads bristled every mile north and south and side roads off of them, and adjacent to each road, bare brown earth.

Hardwoods had been taken from the virgin tropical forest across an area of more than twenty thousand square miles—the surface equivalent of five Floyd

Counties—just in this one operation alone! I think of this disappeared habitat now as I watch the south-migrating warblers out my window. Many of them are bound for tropical forests. I fear it will be a hungry winter for them there, and some will never make it back to Virginia. I wonder if the winter season itself will be altered in coming years, as far more tropical forest trees are removed than are replanted.

One thing Google Earth will show you as well: there are still remote and beautiful places left on the planet to explore—including the mountains and forests of southwest Virginia. Many regions of the world still have sizable patches of sustainable forest, prairie or jungle wilderness intact. We've learned much in the last fifty years about how Earth's ecosystems and creatures get along, and at times, we have created ways to conserve and protect them.

But our numbers on Earth continue to grow and humanity's material and energy needs seem inexhaustible, while the little blue ball is finite. Both the planet's immensity and variety and its susceptibility to the uses and misuses of civilization become more real when you see them with your own eyes from above. "Oh, I've been there!" I say when I read about the melting glaciers of Nepal or the remote lakes of China where bird flu was found recently in wild geese.

Maps orient us to place. Google Earth does this especially well for me. In its three-dimensionality and interactivity it makes me, in a sense, a participant in those places. The global browser as a mapping tool gives the user a literal grounding to the environmental and human stories that unfold in natural landscapes around the world. We are affected more than ever by events that happen on the dark side of our daytime world. They are closer to us than we imagine. I encourage you to go see for yourself.

The New Physics of Firewood
Body and Soul Together

While the implications of the cold, calculating engineering term "efficiency" makes my skin crawl in some cases, in our private economy here on Goose Creek and at this chapter of our lives, producing the greatest product for the least input of effort is something we must think about more and more. This grudging homage to efficiency most especially has to do this time of year with what it will take to stay warm this winter and those to come.

We first started heating with wood in the mid-seventies. On moving from balmy 'bama to Virginia, we couldn't keep the kids warm with oil heat, even at seventeen cents a gallon. A Fisher Momma Bear came into our home.

Ann and I thought nothing then of bucking up a ten-inch standing-dead oak with a bow saw and axe. The fact that we'd have to haul each piece up from a rocky ravine three hundred yards from the hatchback barely entered our minds. Effort was half the fun; the energy in the stacked cord wood couldn't touch the energy expended in its cutting and gathering.

But with all that, a good bit of our hard-earned wood heat went back into the neighborhood through the single pane window glass and uninsulated ceiling of our drafty old rambler on Withers Road in Wytheville. We'd just cut more wood.

That was then, this is now, and as B. B. King sings it, the thrill is gone. While the comfort of wood heat lives on, those early macho-romantic notions about heating with wood cut by my own hands are giving way to more practical considerations.

Even so, there will inevitably be some fallen and standing-dead resources that are bigger in girth than my splitting threshold of eight inches. I can hardly leave these solid trunks to become a slow meal for the organisms of decay. With careful attention to the wood-chopping ergonomics befitting a late fifty-something physical therapist, I still split a fair share each winter using the little-known method that has saved my shins, back and rotator cuff to burn wood yet another year.

In the way of giving you at least one take-home useful lesson from your reading here, let me share this technique with you, and in so doing, pass on a rural household hint that might make some difference in your country living and future orthopedic health.

Take two old tires. Wrap some wire or stout nylon twine around them in several places to keep them one atop the other. Put a single big round or several smaller rounds into the well created by the tires. You'll soon discover the efficiency and wisdom of this method.

The split wood stays in the ring and does not leave manly scars on your shins. The split wood stays standing on end, reducing the distance that the sore back and legs must lower the hands to grasp and lift the splits of wood. The ring helps reduce the arc that the shoulders must follow to complete the split, and the rubber of the tire yields and rebounds, absorbing some of the blow's impact at the end.

There is a creeping ambivalence in our relationship each year with the chain saw, splitting maul and black plastic in the wind. Staying warm some future winter may become a matter of turning up a dial. Perhaps the heat pump cometh, but not today, not this year when we have enough in the stacks to see us through 'til April. We have our health, mostly, and we have Advil. And there will likely be windfalls yet to come.

A Nose for Winter
Within These Walls

Anyone walking Virginia's fields and forests in winter might easily forget they even have a sense of smell. The olfactory world of the cold months can seem a trackless desert for the nose. And yet, if you make a point of it and know where to look, you can find ways to use your sense of smell, even on the coldest winter day.

On our walks along Goose Creek, we're never far from a twig of spicebush. Scratched with the thumbnail, a dormant nose will wake up to an antiseptic smell with overtones of clove and cinnamon. And if I whittle a small branch of yellow birch up along the forest path, it will smell just like teaberry gum, even on the grayest of February days.

We make a point to sample fragrant plants like these as a kind of smelling salts; they jostle our senses back to life in the monochrome hibernation of midwinter.

But it is the inconspicuous remnants of a small plant called Pennyroyal that I search for on a raw February day. The musty aroma of this little mint in winter reaches deepest into that place in my mind where fragrance and memory live intimately together. I've smelled this skeletal wildflower when there was snow on the ground, and the emotional power it holds on me once brought me to tears.

We had left Wytheville in 1987 and returned to my home town of Birmingham. I quickly became immersed in fourteen-hour days of classes and labs. I was soon as absorbed and unreachable to myself as I have ever been, retreating into a single-mindedness of purpose that comes to a man who knows that if he looks down even briefly from the precarious balance in all he has taken on, he will surely fall.

But in a rare moment that year living away from mountains, I slowed down enough one day to pull from the shelf near my desk a personal book, not a text—a natural history simply called *The Appalachians*. It fell open effortlessly across my lap to a page marked by a pressed plant: penny-royal from back home—a stow-away from a place, a time and a personal identity that by then, I could barely remember having lived.

I lifted the flattened sprig from between the pages with some hesitation, knowing where it would carry me. I crushed a small whorl of tiny drab flowers between my fingers and was transported back to a place I had tried so hard to put out of my mind. I recalled it clearly: we used to put little pieces of pennyroyal on the wood stove and its musty sweetness filled the house. How could I ever forget those times?

Often on walks in the Virginia hills when the children were small, I secretly plucked the dry whorls of Pennyroyal from the bank of a favorite trail. Later on, concealed in my cupped hands, I stuck it under their noses for a sniff. "What is it?" I asked them, knowing they knew the answer.

Their reply was usually silly—the name of a bird or salamander—just to pretend they couldn't be bothered to remember dad's silly nature lore. But they remembered: the sense of smell and power of memory saw to that. And I remembered too well, with a lump in my throat as I placed the pressed plant back between pages of a book about mountains I had loved and left.

And to which we have now thankfully returned for good.

And even now, on a bleak gray day in the middle of winter, to smell this mousey little plant crushed against the palm of my hand is a sacrament of belonging. Even in winter, this place just smells like home.

And listen: how very Appalachian, this thunder...in our mountain valley, a discourse, declaration and rebuttal, ridge beyond ridge. Appreciative and silent, we take our empty bowls inside.

10

Grace, Descending
Earth Companions

Red-tailed hawks nest in our Goose Creek valley in the summers, and we hear them so frequently overhead that sometimes we don't even bother to look up. But on a recent summer day, had I allowed that shrill and ordinary call to go unacknowledged, I would have missed a most extraordinary performance in a biology watcher's lifetime.

High up against white cumulus, a pair of red-tails rode the thermals above the rocky tailbone of the ridge where it meets the creek. One bird traced a wide path at four hundred feet, the other, at eight hundred or more. They circled in opposite directions in a single rising kettle of warm air, each aware of the other—probably male and female. The lower bird called its rasping tee-DEEER! and as if in response, the higher bird tucked its wings tight against its body and plummeted straight for the tallest white pines along the ridge line. At the last instant, he pulled out nonchalantly to climb the warm air again and soar in lazy spirals above his partner.

I've watched redtails perform this power dive before, and it always thrills me. For a moment, I become the bird I'm watching, I see what it sees and feel what it feels, falling. My head swims as I pull out of the dive, climbing once more, to look down on the tiny white house where the man stands looking up, shading his eyes with his hand.

But that man had never witnessed the display that followed moments later. The two raptors flew circles together in close formation in an ordinary kind of way, when the one broke free alone to his higher berth. And then, from a great height, the higher raptor tucked his wings. His silhouette against bright cloud became the wingless fuselage of a falling missile, a feathered arrow. The trajectory anticipated the wide sweep of his partner along her slow circle.

At the very last instant in this startling and inexplicable attack, the perfect line of the free-falling bird veered just enough to miss its target. The nearness of his passing pulled his victim sideways into the turbulent undercurrent of his fall. Just then, he unfurled his wings full, breaking his descent, and rose just enough that the two birds were suddenly side by side. And they embraced.

Talon in talon, wings wide and fixed, they fell—yet not a fall, but a dance, a sacrament, each bird for and with the other. A russet, feathered carousel twirled with the smooth spinning fall of a maple fruit in slow motion, in a giddy centripetal act of play or thanksgiving. Round and round through the buoyant air, their outstretched wings traced circles in space and they held to each other for life, for joy, in graceful descent. At the last moment, they parted as if nothing out of the ordinary had happened, and resumed their silent scribes in the thermal over the ridge.

Was this performance practiced or spontaneous? Was it a ritual, fixed by instinct or a creative and cooperative act of will? My inner poet even considered for the briefest moment that perhaps these two birds chose to do this aerial ballet there and then because I had acknowledged their presence by looking up, and I had been an honored and appreciative audience of one.

I know better, of course. But having seen this, I will be more inclined to expect small and private miracles of beauty in the years that remain. And I will ponder the likelihood that we create these revelations simply by being receptive and ready for them in the ordinary of our busy lives.

Things I Like About Summer
Not Fish Nor Fowl

Getting out of bed wearing boxer shorts, period. Not two pair of socks, silk long johns, sweatpants, T-shirt, sweatshirt and fleece sweater—the typical Winter straight-out-of-bed garb.

Getting out of bed and going straight to the coffee pot. I don't have to go out on the porch where it is obscenely dark and obscenely cold in all the February garb mentioned above to get kindling to start the fire. No crumpling newspaper, wiping soot off the sleeve of my fleece sweater. In summer I don't bang my knuckles on the wood stove door pulling singed digits back from a smouldering fire that all of a sudden leaps into a conflagration, the July sun up close and personal.

Sitting on the front porch with a cup of coffee in the mornings. Maybe two cups. Listening to the quiet sounds of creek and a gentle wind, the steam from my cup rising in a shaft of morning sun.

The warmth of the morning sun on my bare legs, while sitting on the front porch after coffee, listening to the quiet sounds of nature, holding a good book in my hands which are not covered in soot.

The warmth of the morning sun on a vine-ripened tomato eaten whole in the garden, just after my first cup of morning coffee and a chapter of a good book.

The smells that rise from the warm earth, wafting on the morning sun, the smell of pollen and petals, lilacs, yellow sweet clover, spearmint along the creek, damp loam...the smell of coffee and of ripe tomatoes.

Seeing from the garden the orderly rows of stacked firewood seasoning behind the house, waiting for a month when the sun's scorching heat is only a uncomfortable memory, its pleasant warmth a fleeting rarity; in the weak heat of January sun, the sour smell of oak, the medicinal smell of walnut, and the sweet smell of cherry. Each piece in the stack from woodlot to face cord has been touched over and over by these hands that will in a few short months crumple newspaper and offer each piece of wood I'd cut into the stove like an sacrament, while my mind thinks back on how nice it was to be warm, to smell the earth, to live in my skin alone, to have experienced Summer.

October Homecoming: Finding Virginia
Local Color

Our resolve was firm and hope of finding home was strong. The time was right in October, 1974, a year we would cross a geographic portal into the future of our young lives. Octobers since have been at month to think back, the time of year we discovered that Virginia would be where we belonged in this world. On a damp, calm morning this week, the fragrant decay of leaves on our gravel road brought that tale of our northern migration back full to memory.

"Why don't you come up and spend a few days, and we'll canoe the New River" offered my best friend from Auburn who had just started a PhD program at Virginia Tech. "You'll love the mountains up here" he said without a trace of doubt. Perhaps he saw back then what I've only recently discovered about myself: that I am Appalachian and the mountains are my true center. I belong in them, and always have.

But Virginia has mountains? I remember thinking to myself as I pulled the Rand-McNally from the shelf to find the town and the river I'd soon be visiting.

Through Chattanooga, Knoxville, Bristol, the road would carry me north. I'd always imagined Virginia to be rolling hills dotted with cattle and grazing horses, like Alabama's coastal plain.

And I'd never heard of this south-to-north river—a major river, I was told—and sure enough, there it was on the map, cutting north across the contours through the very backbone of the Appalachians along the West Virginia line.

This trip was well-timed. Ann and I had decided that we wouldn't stay in my home town of Birmingham to raise our year-old daughter. Increasingly we were called to a country homestead of our imaginations, the vision made clearer by our reading of *Mother Earth News* and a book called *"Finding and Buying Your Place in the Country."*

"I want a house on a creek, a two story white farmhouse with double porches" Ann dreamed out loud. She could see in her mind's eye what it would look like, but not where it would be. She was bound to dream that same dream for exactly thirty-five years.

So I would go up and canoe the New with my friend Ed alright, but I would also interview for jobs on the way home, so the trip would be about more than just me having a good time. Still, with the soured economy of the early 70s, a recent Middle East oil embargo and veterans returning to get the federal postings, the odds of finding a job were stacked against me. Even so, I had hope that when I got back to Birmingham from that trip to Blacksburg, I might have a clearer idea of where we were going next in the short story of our lives.

I could hear the theme song from Route 66 playing in my head as I left town at daybreak on my existential odyssey along that lonesome stretch of road between home and the Tennessee line. Rocky canyons rimmed the north Alabama valley highway, and like pointing fingers of the southern Appalachians, they directed my way northeast. Fall's colors and temperatures grew more vibrant and invigorating the further north I drove toward Chattanooga. Life was good and getting better by the mile.

Even distant horizons had sharp edges that October day. And after finally crossing the state line into Virginia, I caught an occasional glimpse of high and nameless ridge tops far away—what I now know as Rogers, Iron, Glade and Walker Mountains. My heart soared. If only we could settle in a place like this! I wanted Ann to see and share all of it, because she'd feel the same pull toward these mountains and forests, I was sure.

Late that afternoon after ten hours on the road I pulled my little Datsun into the parking lot at my friends' apartment in Blacksburg. The next day on a fog-chilly autumn morning, Ed and I put the canoe in at McCoy Falls (this was a much bigger and more powerful river than I'd imagined!) and we took out several hours later at the Eggleston bridge.

On the way home, in a thinly-veiled attempt to entice his college buddy to move his family closer, Ed drove me around the pleasant back roads of Montgomery County where every turn was more picturesque than anything I'd seen in the Alabama countryside. I was attracted, infatuated, then smitten by Virginia (which is, after all, for lovers) but I would need more than the pull of strong emotion if I was to commit to forever in the Commonwealth. I would need an income.

The next day on campus, while I was waiting for my friend to get out of class at Tech, I spotted a most auspicious job posting on the bulletin board outside his classroom. It stopped me in my tracks: Wytheville Community College— biology instructor, need is immediate, masters degree preferred.

I had made a solo journey to Virginia to visit friends, canoe and explore with little hope to return home triumphantly to wife and baby daughter with a job. And then out of the blue, came this possibility—in October, an odd time in the academic year to be filling a slot in a college biology department. I'd pass right by the place on my way home. I knew better than to set my hopes too high, but it looked as though Providence had placed this gift before me and at just the right time.

I had to remind myself that back home in our Birmingham apartment, a wall was papered with rejection letters from little colleges just like this one. Why did I think the outcome for this teaching position was going to be any different? And yet, I did believe it, and powerfully, with an eerie confidence that this job was as good as mine.

A few days later, I departed Blacksburg, my first stop an hour west: Wytheville Community College. I pulled my little car into visitor parking and walked confidently onto campus wearing the best of my rugged but clean trekking and canoeing garb, with great and naïve expectations. (Drat! I discovered I had left my interview clothes hanging on the door of our apartment in Alabama! I'd have to interview in hiking boots.)

After a two hour meeting, I was still in the running for the position, but one candidate of many. Before I left campus, I found the empty faculty office that might someday be mine. Through the window and the eye of faith I saw me sitting with my feet propped on that desk—my desk—reading through class notes just before a lecture. Could this be the future I was seeing, or merely another mirage?

As I drove south from Wytheville that day, those anonymous ridges and creeks I'd seen from the interstate on my October journey to Virginia became mine on the trip back to Alabama. This country had taken possession of me and it felt like home; southwest Virginia was where in the world we were supposed to be. Of that I was certain—of this job to get us there, less so.

And then we waited for the call. And waited. Two weeks seemed like forever. But come, it did—and in the first week of November, Ann and I retraced my steps north, together, hopeful. By then, the leaves were going drab. The golden hillsides I'd seen in October were shades of rust and raw sienna, beautiful but subdued and almost somber.

I'd been studying the maps, so when we reached Marion, I took Route 16 to Route 42—the Old Wilderness Road—along the Holston, and east through

Rich Valley. It was like going back in time, so very different from Birmingham's busy suburbs. At Sharon Springs, we climbed up out of the valley on a little road so small it could have been someone's driveway. And on that day it was utterly carpeted in newly-fallen leaves, as if the Fates had strewn rose petals to welcome us. In both our minds, it was exactly here that we knew we had arrived. The next day, the job was mine, and we would be transplanted to these hills for good.

A week before Christmas, we pulled that little Datsun behind a small U-haul truck that contained all our worldly possessions. We carried it piece by piece to an upstairs apartment on Spiller Street in Wytheville—a rental someone at the college had set up for us, sight unseen. We remarked what a quiet place it was that first night, only to discover when they returned from the holidays that below us lived a family whose denomination put great stock in the importance of procreation. We bought our first house on Withers Road in town (quiet but cold!) not long thereafter.

My first day as a faculty member—me, the kid, the marginally employed biologist, teaching!—was January 6, 1975. And for the next twelve years, I propped my feet on that same desk until the summer of 1987 when we left, paradoxically, to return to Birmingham from whence we had come so long ago. And in '89, with a two year MS completed, we escaped once more to the mountains, but in North Carolina this time. After all, mountains are mountains, we thought.

But something wasn't right. We had by then owned houses in many places in the sight of mountains, but for some reason, only felt home in Virginia's hills. And so when our nest was about to empty in the mid nineties, we began to think of migrating back this way. My hopes (as a hiker, photographer and botanist) were, this time, to settle in the Blue Ridge versus Wythe County's ridges and valleys. And when we drove through Floyd—by chance or providence—for the first time in the summer of 1995, I had that same sense of certainty I'd had when I saw that job posting on the board at Tech: the place is right, the time is right, and we belong here.

And every October and November, I remember the itinerary through time and across geography that brought us just here. The smell of fallen leaves, the dazzling blue of sky that follows an autumn cold front, the slow roads that wind through these old mountains that are in all the world unique—these sights and sounds recall the best of memories of those autumn days of traveling hopefully north, to arrive, finally, at home: a house on a creek, a two story white farmhouse with double porches.

Front Porch View of Floyd County Spring
Local Color

The coming of spring at our house is not measured by length of day or temperature. It is not the blooming of Coltsfoot (come far too early this year) or pinking of the buds at the tips of trees along Nameless Creek that signals spring to us. The first day of spring at my house is marked by the afternoon or evening of our first meal of the year on the front porch.

This year, it was she—the irresistible force—who insisted: let's eat outside! And I—the pseudo-immovable object: it's too cool yet, and everything is wet from the rain. But there's a break in the storm, the air warms suddenly, but more rain is coming.

It is chilly for sitting, but she insists. I relent, and a flannel shirt for the evening is just enough. Before she comes to sit, I stand and listen. Beneath the raucous sound of the creek, spring hums underground. I feel it through my slippers, in the soles of my feet.

This month is to June as early morning is to noon: there is not much color or warmth yet in the day or the year. But the sun rises sooner and stays longer, beaming layers of pigment onto the diluted palette of February. The late March breeze carries the earth-sweet scent of warming soil, tousles the spindly spice-bush just starting to bud along the creek.

The pasture grass is smooth as a putting green painted butterscotch, pressed down by winter, flat as pancake batter. Five black crows move erratically back and forth across the field like ice skaters, leaning forward, arms tight against their sides, gliding in the twin choreography of hunger and curiosity. There is a blessed peace in watching this panorama from the stage of our own front porch.

In bowls on our laps, the casserole (with the chicken we canned ourselves last fall) warms us even while the winds follow the storm south, down beyond the end of the pasture, surging like a wave out across the Blue Ridge, spilling down into the piedmont and beyond. Behind the wave, a neon strobe of pink flashes in the near-dark. Thunder follows by and by, the sluggish complaint of the instant light and heat that spoke it. There: the smell of lightning.

And listen: how very Appalachian, this thunder. Remember: in South Dakota, the storm passed over us, crashing it's way toward the Badlands. For being so very close and loud, it was but a brief exclamation, monotone and two dimensional—a sheet of sound dropped down hard against prairie, flat and open to the horizon in every direction. In our mountain valley, thunder is a discourse, declaration and rebuttal, ridge beyond ridge.

CLAP! And we hold to our warm bowls, listening. Mountain Thunder in stereo, reverberating with more than mere percussion: antiphonal thunder kettle drums answered by two or more pairs of tympanis back on Lick Ridge, set at fifths. Tonal heavy hammers strike steel against steel out beyond Copper Hill. Sound sent out and back again, modulated, amplified, and moving away. The pink-orange cumulus spills down the great escarpment toward Carolina as Goose Creek rises clear and cold, to its own water music.

Appreciative and filled, we take our empty bowls inside.

The Long Way Home
For the Time, Being

I don't think it would have been any harder to leave one of the children behind when we moved away. I know that parting with our dog was one of the most agonizing decisions I have ever had to make. This is Zachary's story. We forsook him out of practical necessity. He found us out of canine determination, unwavering love and by means of forces and reckoning we will never understand.

Ann and the children and I moved from our rural home in Virginia in 1987 so that I could retrain for a new career. It meant leaving behind our best friend, Zachary, a six year old Black Lab. This was for his good; he would be miserable penned up in suburban Birmingham while we were away from home every day. We all agreed that he should remain free to roam and explore the countryside. We found friends of friends, far across the county, over a mountain, beyond the interstate.

They would be glad to give him a new home. He trembled beside me as I drove him there. And I left him tearfully, watching him on his new front porch, disappearing in the distance of the rear view mirror. I tried feebly to convince myself that old Zach did not really care who cared for him. He would be fine and we would soon outgrow our mutual loss.

A year later, in our new home in a Birmingham suburb, we got a call from the people who bought our farmhouse back near Wytheville. Ann took the phone; the color drained from her face as the kids and I watched the conversation unfold. Our callers told Ann "There's a strange dog showed up here a couple days ago. He's a big black dog, and he stays under the porch here. He's right thin and his paws don't look so good. He just seems sort of lost and confused. The neighbors down the road say they think he's your old dog." We made more calls and confirmed the truth of this otherworldly resurrection.

"It's Zachary and he found his way home. He's looking for us and Fred, you have to go get him" Ann said through tears of joy and remorse. I knew she was right.

We had to go. But bringing Zachary there to Birmingham made no more sense than it would have a year earlier. Even so, the next day, driven by forces beyond reason, my daughter and I drove ten hours to our old farmhouse.

And it was Zach for sure, though less of him than we had left, and he was confused when he first saw us. There was some white hair among the black now; he had become prematurely old at seven doggy years. But as he recognized us, he responded to all of the commands he once obeyed, as if we had never been apart.

How often we have wished that this was a world where dogs could talk. He could tell us how he made it twenty miles across a mountain range, a very busy interstate, and down many country roads through unfamiliar territory, to home. And then, when he finally arrived back at the farm, we weren't there. What he must have thought and felt!

It was obvious that his travels had taken him months. And yet he had persisted, driven by the need to find his pack, his neck-huggers and stick-throwers and playmates; his family. It was not enough to get these things from the substitute family of strangers who treated him well enough, but were not his. To find his true home must have been a driving need in his mind from that first week with his counterfeit family. He waited and waited, finally knowing one day that I was not coming back for him and he would have to make the trip back to us on his own.

Zach stayed with us through two more moves—to Sylva and Morganton, North Carolina; but he never made it back to Virginia. At age 12, elderly in dog years, he had become decrepit, uncomfortable and incontinent. Each day was a misery for him. We made the decision to send him out of this world painlessly. Of course, it was a very hard thing to do.

But looking back, I see that euthanasia was an easier decision than the one we made to leave our good friend with strangers, thinking he would never see us again, and knowing he would never rest until he found us.

Walking the Talk: Wayward Virginian
For the Time, Being

I wrote the first and last of this four-part true tale collaboration, the middle two parts were written by our son Nathan for a four part "special to the press" serial in the Floyd paper. You'll read here just the dust jacket of a long journey home story in which we all participated; all of us exhausted several Big Angels, but only one of us wore out two pair of boots and lived for weeks off dry Ramen noodles and honey.

When our son, Nathan, brought home a 1940s-vintage manual typewriter at Thanksgiving break our first autumn here on Goose Creek, our curiosity was aroused. The muffled tick-tick-ching of the keys and carriage return upstairs jangled late into the night, long after the old folks had gone to bed. What could be going on with him?

Just before he left to go back to college, we learned his plan (we suspected that he might have a plan): to take a semester off that year; to find a cabin on a frozen lake he imagined in the far north (Canada someplace, he said—what his plan possessed in enthusiasm it lacked in particulars) and to write a book.

The memory of those days comes to me easily now; it was this time of year—in the bleak mid-winter of 2000—that we reluctantly wished him God speed, waved goodbye and sent him off for Maine, as he would have it no other way. The plan had finally morphed into this final form: he would take the ferry from Bar Harbor over to Nova Scotia some months later in the spring when the ice broke up.

There, he would hike the entire coast of the island, and write about that experience. At least that is what he lead us to think his journey would be about, and we could plainly see the cost of this hole in his college career. Only he alone could see then all that was to be gained from it.

He found a barely-heated attic room for rent in Bar Harbor and took a job in a local deli there in town. On his days off, he hiked the mountains and shorelines of Arcadia National Park. In the dead of winter, he had it pretty much had it all to himself. Every couple of weeks, we got a request for first one bit, then another of my hiking and camping gear. He'd never shown that much interest in backpacking before, but of course now, he'd need it for Nova Scotia.

And as the first of April arrived, he called us to explain what he really intended. The horror.

"Mom, dad, I'm not going to hike Nova Scotia after all. What I'm going to do—and I know you'll tell me a hundred good reasons why this is a crazy idea, and I don't blame you but you just gotta trust me on this, I know it's what I'm meant to do—I'm going to hike home along the back roads from one small village or town to the next, every step from Bar Harbor to Goose Creek."

Stiffing wails of protest, his mother and I exchanged stunned and disbelieving gazes from our respective phones. Nate continued, with our full attention.

"I'm going to cast my fate on the kindness of strangers and show America that there are still good people in this country, caring and trusting people who will take me in and show hospitality to a kid just passing through. I'll not be taking the Appalachian Trail—except maybe a little through New York and New Jersey."

"If nobody offers to put me up for the night, dad, I have your tent and backpack and lots of warm clothes. And if there's ever anything I don't have and need, I'll never be more than a hour or so away from a phone, and I'll call you and tell you what post office to send it to. I've thought it all through. I'm not an idiot. Besides, it's spring. I'll be fine. You'll see."

We were far from convinced, but with our only son a thousand miles from home, we offered him as much support as our parental angst would allow. With no small despair, we prayed for road angels and good Samaritans. We waited every day that first week for his calls as we anticipated his progress south on the map from Maine, step by small step.

But to return safely home would take tens of thousands of steps—down empty, nameless roads, past junk-yard dogs and pickup trucks with gun racks in the back window with near-misses by reckless drivers; breathing exhaust fumes; hungry, exposed to the cold, wet wind and lost. We imagined the worst. What did he imagine? What did he know about the world and would his naiveté and trust be his undoing?

After writing this first couple of paragraphs, I called Nate in Missouri (yes, he survived) and convinced him that he owed his long-suffering parents a retro-spective as to what had been going on in his young mind as he concocted and carried out his hair-brained idiot's dream. He agreed to write. And so for the next two installments here, I will sit back and let him tell his side of the story. This should be interesting.

In his last installment of "A Road Less Traveled" [the author's Floyd Press column] my dad reflected back on the origins of some of his more treasured gray hairs. In particular, he was thinking of a dumb stunt I pulled—a road that I traveled—eight years ago when I'd just turned 21.

I had recently developed an obsession with all things Northern. North for me, was no mere cardinal direction. It was, instead, a fabled place where adventure thrived. Somewhere up north, and soon, I'd move into some blustery hut and write bad poetry and eat snow till spring. Then, plump on whale-blubber and weeks of cheap wine, my real adventure would begin. I would wander to the roadside, put out my thumb, and like a poem scrawled on the back of a napkin, I'd blow away.

With Mom and Dad waving handkerchiefs behind me in Floyd that January of 2000, I drove a thousand miles northbound to Bar Harbor, Maine. For the next three blizzard-ridden months, I holed up in an attic and did a lot of the safe, sane things I promised Mom and Dad I would do. I brushed my teeth; I slept indoors (and sometimes in my car). I worked at a deli a couple doors down. And on the wilder fringes of things, I hiked Mount Desert Island for hours a day. And back in my room, I wrote hundreds of pages of excited babble that all boiled down to three words: Youth! Life! Possibility!

Dad seems to think that all along I was secretly scheming to walk back home to Floyd. But here he gives me too much credit. In fact, at that point, the idea had never yet crossed my mind. What I conceived early on was less a "plan" than a recipe: no money, no agenda, just an open road and a willingness for… well, whatever.

But on April Fool's Day (fittingly enough) I put all these other ideas on hold. Late that night, wandering alone on a pitch-black road a few miles outside of Bar Harbor, I stopped with exhaustion and laid down, looking up at a frigid, starry sky. And there, feeling my body heat leach into the asphalt, I knew that my plans had changed. I would have no more visions of hitched rides and freight trains: these only made the roadsides a blur. I wanted to see everything—the good, bad and sprawl alike—and that meant moving slowly, taking it in with every step. I had driven from Virginia to Maine in two days, and since had forgotten nearly all of it. I knew I wouldn't forget a walk back home.

Ten days later, I hefted my dad's creaky old Jansport on my back and headed out of Bar Harbor. I could still hear Mom's voice ringing in my ears—recounting on the phone, the day before, how much she'd cried, how little she and Dad had slept in the last week, how sure they both were that I'd "learn the hard way" the fallen state and dangers of a modern world.

That night of the first day on the road, with some twenty miles now behind me, I was hiking, yet again on a pitch-black road. The occasional headlights of logging trucks flashed through sleet and freezing rain. Each time a truck roared past, I stumbled to the roadside, often into puddles, my eyes forced down by the light's blinding glare in the blackness.

This time, I had no attic to return to, and a warm bed in Virginia was still some thousand miles away. What on earth had I done? At one point, a passing pair of headlights silhouetted a roadside picnic table just ahead. Ready for any relief, I fished out my flashlight and hurried to the table. "No Camping" read the sign nearby.

At this point, I didn't care. Gathering a small heap of fallen branches, I put a small pile between myself and the road, and covered my pack with the rest. Under the table, I climbed clumsily into my sleeping bag, and prayed for sleep.

For the next two weeks, as I walked my first two hundred miles toward New Hampshire, many of Mom and Dad's lesser fears were realized. The temperature seldom rose above 35 degrees, and ten days of rain sought to kill me before I ever left Maine. There was also plenty of the foretold bad traffic, sprawl, and even some butt-nipping dogs, sure enough.

But what none of us expected—myself included—was the outpouring of kindness from the roadsides. In the first twelve days on the road, nine different strangers took me in. And suddenly I realized that my long walk home would be far less about the days walking and more about the late evenings talking with monks, cowgirls, and dying old tycoons.

In the month it took to walk through New England, you might have thought I'd have gotten wiser for the wear.

In Connecticut, after a few hundred miles of back roads, I decided that I'd try out the Appalachian Trail. Nothing stupid there: New York and New Jersey loomed ahead, and taking the Trail was a good way of skirting the sprawl.

But after a week alone in the woods, I started feeling rugged and self-sufficient. With grim excitement, I mailed home my sleeping bag, hat, gloves, and sweater. I needed nothing! I was Nate of the Wild.

And then came the cold front. For the next several days, the sky turned gray, temperatures plummeted, and a cold rain made relentless, baneful raids on my underwear.

By the time I crossed the New Jersey border, the weather had taken its toll. I was hypothermic. My lips and fingertips were blue; my hands were losing their coordination. My shaking was sometimes more akin to convulsion, and sometimes stopped altogether. By then, instinct had finally kicked in. I was even ready to break my "no hotels" rule. Trouble was, the closest hotel was still a day's walk away.

That night I shared a shelter with "Pops," a 60-year-old who had planned to hike northbound into Massachusetts. His plans, though, had changed. Tomorrow, he promised, he'd be home bound, to all things warm and dry.

Pops was far from cheery. "You ready to freeze your butt off tonight?"

I just nodded grimly. At times Pops and I tried to talk ourselves into distraction. Other times one of us would say good night and plunge in, hoping that we were ready for sleep and the morning would come quickly.

Finally, well after dark, a crashing down the trail startled us from our chattering little worlds. Flashlights flung out across wet trees along the ridge. "Who in the heck could that be?" said Pops in disbelief. "What time is it, anyway?" I looked at my watch. "Eight thirty."

Pops moaned. "I've been in this shelter since noon today. Been in my sleeping bag since five ..." He mumbled off. "... damn thought it was at least one o'clock." We whistled to the oncoming hikers to let them know they'd found the place. They whooped back.

One was singing. Pops quietly growled.

Rich and Ed unpacked their things and we all got acquainted. They were leaders of a Boy Scout troop back in town, they said. They'd planned this trip as a reward for their troop, but none of their scouts had been fool enough to come.

"More for us, I guess," said Ed.

Trail Magic: tral-ma-jik. n. A term used commonly by hikers of the Appalachian Trail to signify a moment of overwhelming fortune at the time of greatest need.

Rich lugged a ten-pound propane grill from his pack and set it up in the light drizzle.

"Itellya, Ed, I am starving." Rich looked at the two of us. "What about you boys? Up for a coupla ribeyes?"

Plump, juicy, rib-eye steaks. Sautéed mushrooms and onions. Various hills of scalloped potatoes. Warmth. In a delectable cheesy white sauce with pepper. Trail Magic.

For the time being, let me end with a confession. When I started walking home to Floyd, I thought the trip would be less warmth, less Magic. More me. Alone with the road. Nobody else.

So before I lead you to believe that I "walked off to look for America," a star in some Simon and Garfunkel song, I'll admit that my goals were not really so noble. I didn't entirely expect to meet a whole bunch of Riches and Eds. And without them, frankly, I had little desire to "find America."

If you'll forgive the clichéd way of saying it, though, I think America found me. In countless feats of "Road Magic," America walked off its front porches, stopped me in its front yards, invited me into its homes and offered stories, suppers, hot showers and warm beds. America of all kinds, all shapes and sizes: college kids and brave old ladies; pastors, professors, doctors and farmers. And if that wasn't enough, Ma mailed me cookies, and Dad even came out to join me for a while, and we shared some Trail Magic together. But that's a story I'll let him tell.

"I wonder where I'll sleep tonight and, Lordy, what Fiction lies ahead. By this time tomorrow I could be in anything from three feet of snow to a choir of angels, but I've got some real estate here in my bags." That, from Nate's journal, first night on the road.

And Lordy, how his mom and I tried to trust those angels—that they would keep up his pace and oh please, leave him down here on Earth to grow up beyond his Karouack-y youthful delusions.

Wide-eyed and awake in the wee hours of April 2000, his mother's voice quivered in the dark. "I wonder where Nathan is right now." I couldn't tell her I wished that it was me out there with no obligations but to see what and who would be around each new bend. And yes, I was worried, too.

His unconditional trust was the thing that worried me most. He believed the best of everyone and if he fell, he couldn't image not landing on his feet. That the trip might leave him lost and disoriented wasn't so much a fear as a solemn wish:

"After all, we look around the most when we don't know where we are. And the more we look around the stronger—and more helplessly, wonderfully lost than ever—we become. When a generation gets swallowed up in believing we're not lost, it makes for a youth that's too much like adulthood. Our generation, for instance, has been all too miserably found. Being found has made us sheltered. Being sheltered has made us dull."

That spring I learned the minutiae of New England geography, sending Ann's cookies and more dry socks to post offices in tiny villages along the way. We tried to imagine each night that he would be taken in. He wasn't always.

He learned to face rejection, and small wonder—a long-haired young stranger who appears in the cold rain on the doorstep. He stopped into a country church service one stormy late April evening where the sermon topic was on taking in the needy. How providential, he must have thought. Afterward, they closed up the church and sent him on his way, Lord bless you, son.

Later that same frigid night, miles further down the road, an elderly lady also regretfully told him "no." A half block later, she came running along behind him in her robe and slippers, convicted that it was the right thing to take the risk. A stranger, she took him in, and became his surrogate grandmother and friend for one night over cocoa and cake and conversation.

When he'd lost his way on the Massachusetts Mid-state Trail, four lady hikers gently let him know he was on the opposite side of the mountain from where he thought. They carried him to dinner in town, and late that night, re-deposited him on the trail with a good map, a full stomach, and his trust in trail magic intact.

Each new state line he crossed was a parental prayer answered, though in truth, still hundreds of miles away he might still as well be on the far side of the moon. Then finally, crossing the Potomac, our wayward son was in Virginia. A week or two later, he was at Afton Mountain. We breathed a premature sigh of relief.

He was in high spirits when he left his pack beside the Blue Ridge Parkway and ran off to call us from a nearby house. A half-hour later, his second call was not so cheerful. Clearly, he hadn't hidden his pack well enough. When he went back for it, the pack was gone.

Everything he owned was in that old pack, including his entire journal of the walk. The next day, a Parkway road crew found the old Jansport tossed off in the weeds a mile or two away. Not a thing was missing.

On July 7, 2000, Ann and I joined Nate for the last two miles of his journey down our country lane. The stories poured out: most comforting, some unsettling, but all overflowing with the love of life and language and the heady blind curves of youth. There had been a book in every soul he'd met, in every town, every forest, every new day.

His thick journal that came from the trip is itself a fragmentary recording of 1000 miles of abundant life. These four thumbnail distillations here do scant justice to the richness of the story. Even so, I've appreciated this excuse to collaborate with Nathan, to tell together a bit of our harrowing, ultimately joyful, family adventure. Thank you for letting us share the tale.

We'll Be In This Old House For A While Yet
Within These Walls

When I turned fifty, I claimed with male pride that physically, I could still do pretty much whatever I wanted. My minor aches and pains plus some slight decline in energy and motivation at that round number really didn't slow me down if I set my mind to a task. And at just about that time of life, we found before us the biggest task we'd ever undertaken.

We first laid eyes on this 120-year-old house for sale in northeastern Floyd County in February of 1999. Without the slightest temptation to give it a closer look, I drove on past—a money pit if I'd ever seen one. But she insisted—rightly, as it turns out—that we belonged here. Three days later, we'd bought the farm. The first contractor shared my doubts. He suggested we should offer the house and barn to the local fire department for practice, and build new.

But the house had a sound roof, good ghosts, and a certain unpretentious nobility. We made the decision to sink our teeth (not to mention our life savings) into the massive project of its renovation, knowing that in finding home we ought not defer either gratification or the effort this would take for too many more years. And that chilly May morning in 1999, I stood by as the backhoe took down the outhouse perched where our new "deer-proof" garden now stands.

That demolition marked the beginning of six months of unrelenting labor on behalf of this old house, a test of our wills and of our physical endurance, a ticking clock to "just do it." Now it's done, even with a few extras like the new garden fence and shed. We are almost certainly on the downhill side of the hardest work we will ever do in our lives—a fact the last birthday has written in very large letters.

Turning sixty in April has been a sobering milestone. With this large-ish round number of cycles I've had the sense that we have crested the ridge and started the slow coast toward the end of the line. That we have finally become numerically "old" is a fact I reluctantly accept and will try to be happy for the free coffee at Denny's.

But I had the tiny revelation this morning that maybe I ought not pack my bags just yet. The vision came to me of years future, their numbers filing past me in a receding time line against a cosmic backdrop of black universe. One of those numbers—only God knows which—will be the year I die.

"But Wait. Let's think about the future this way" the morning muse gently offered. "If you live as long as your mother is today, you'll still be around in 2030. If you match your grandmother's age when she died, 2043. There could well be an awful lot of new days ahead for you, sonny boy."

Given those actuarial possibilities of life yet to come, I guess I'd better get back to thinking about what it is I want to do when I grow up. Maybe another book? And certainly, more grandchildren!

Each morning even yet is full of new possibilities. Granted, not all of the choices are available from the menu of ten years ago, but there are surely enough to make the selection an interesting proposition over the morning's coffee.

And you'd think maybe sixty years of experience, skill, perspective and a smattering of wisdom might just be useful for something between now and 2043. To everything there is a season. We'll just have to discover what crops we want to grow in this new season in our lives.

Knowing Your Endive
from Your Escargot

These end-pages weren't absolutely necessary, but I thought it might be a helpful appendix and a way for you to make sense of the "tags" I put below each essay or story in the book so that you would know a bit about its flavor and texture before you dig in. You'll find that the ten Parts of the book are each a mixture of most of these various food groups, offering a stew, a casserole, a blend of tastes. Bon appetit!

I. Curious By Nature: Today's youngest generation stands at risk of becoming completely distanced from the natural world, and this is not okay. Today's cloistered kids are deprived of the nutrients of outdoor play every day and by choice, cocooned indoors, by and large lacking curiosity that leads to learning about the real world under the sky. They may not know the joy of free outdoor play, "protected" as they often are from direct contact with the natural world and the certain risks of learning their physical limits. They need guides back outside. Maybe you do, too. If this is a subject you'd like to explore in more detail, I recommend Richard Louv's *Last Child in the Woods,* a book that goes to some length to understand and successfully address what the author describes as "nature deficit disorder." Also find the Child and Nature Network online.

II. Earth Companions: My first love even as a toddler was nature. "Look mommy!" I called with amazement (I am told) from the front porch step. "A pillowcase!" The disgusted caterpillar just moved on, and fortunately, my taxonomic precision and word retrieval skills improved somewhat over the years. My first graduate education was in zoology, and a major fascination with the plant kingdom came along later, flames fanned by my zeal for wildflower photography. I've been a "biology watcher" since the last Ice Age and it's intricacies and marvels never cease to delight, educate and amaze the little boy that still lives on in me. Nature (yes, even spiders and snakes and "bugs") offers an unending source of wonder and beauty for both pen and camera lens, as well as for the lessons we can learn about life at large. Read here a few lightly-illuminating cameos of a sampling of the creatures we live with (for good or ill) in Southwest Virginia.

III. Within Our Means: Heads up! This file cabinet of varied topical focus looks particularly at the adult of our species and the choices we make. These essays are issues-centered, often with local reference, on subjects including invasive plants, the roadside scourge of the plastic bag, and the central community issue of water. Here-and-now matters like these are not made irrelevant to a wider readership by placing them on our small stage and at a particular point in time. (Paper or plastic? Surely you've wondered.)

IV. Not Fish Nor Fowl: Now don't tell me otherwise. I know you have a drawer at your house just like we have at ours. It is near the kitchen phone. You don't open it when company comes or they'll see a rat's nest of grocery receipts, the last two or three sheets of a dozen different pastel sticky note pads, dog-eared from being crumpled in purse and pocket; some Green Stamps collected in the past millennium; point-broken pencils, out of ink ball points, a few dog treats and some pocket lint, all held together by a tangle of paper clips. This, dear reader, is that drawer of hard to label odds and ends.

V. Local Color: These selections have to with being at home, celebrating and probing the idea that we belong in some sense to the places where we live our lives, young and old. As is the case for so much of the rest of this collection, these pieces take different vantages points—looking down, looking up, looking out—for a better view of what we hold in our hands.

VI. Body and Soul Together: This assortment of earthy pieces has to do mostly with two components of the "food, clothing and shelter" triangle of necessities of life: staying fed and staying warm. Gardening and gathering the winter wood from the forest on our place are time-and-energy intensive chores with the ultimate purpose of maintaining enough body heat to keep body and soul together. And in the process, we sometimes get more exercise and excitement than we bargained for, and learn some difficult but memorable life lessons.

VII. Within These Walls: What takes place within these walls and within the perimeter of our "owned" boundaries here in rural Virginia would be a private matter, were it not for my fairly newly-acquired affliction of turning the personal into the public by writing out the sublime or silly stories of everyday life. As the name suggests, these come more from our Department of the Interior.

VIII. For the Time, Being: The pieces in this final drawer have to do with special people along the trail—including poems from and about our kids, a gift of memories to and from my mother, the peregrinations of our first family dog and a shared family adventure. There is a veiled memoir of sorts woven through the book, and this section tends in more that direction that some of the others, with the recurrent theme of the years surging through us as we hold our place in time.

About the Author

Fred First is a lifelong biology watcher, photographer and teacher, with MS degrees in vertebrate zoology and physical therapy. In 2002, Fred temporarily left his former professions and began to write from his home in the remote corner of a rural Virginia county.

Since then, he has recorded more than two dozen essays for broadcast on the Roanoke NPR station, WVTF. He writes a biweekly column called *The Road Less Traveled* for the Floyd Press. His photographs have been used widely, recently including the National Geographic affiliated site, Landscope America. He credits his webblog, *Fragments from Floyd,* for the discipline of daily writing that generated first book, *Slow Road Home: a Blue Ridge Book of Days* (which is still available) and now *What We Hold In Our Hands: a Slow Road Reader.*

In addition to his writing and photography, Fred is involved part-time in physical therapy practice in a nearby clinic. When he isn't teaching, treating patients or writing, he enjoys gardening, natural history, digital photography and—as long as his joints hold up to it—gathering the firewood to heat their restored farm house on Goose Creek. Fred and Ann have two grown children, two grand daughters, and always at least one Labrador retriever.

Email Fred at fred1st@gmail.com for comments, questions or requests for books, notecards or as speaker at your organization or event. Order forms are provided at the end of the book and on the websites. Find out the latest at Fred's blog, fragmentsfromfloyd.com or book web site SlowRoadHome.com.

Need more books? An order form is provided here, and please visit the websites for additional copies.

Goose Creek Press

~ Please send this page with your order ~
Items will be mailed to you promptly upon receipt

ITEM	VALUE	TOTALS
Books		
Slow Road Home	_____@ *$16	_____
What We Hold...	_____@ $18	_____
Notecards		
Blue Ridge Country	_____ @ $10	_____
Blue Ridge Parkway	_____ @ $10	_____
Blue Ridge Autumn	_____ @ $10	_____
Glimpses of Floyd	_____@ $10	_____
	SUBTOTAL =	_____

Please add $1.25 for each set of notecards and $3.00 for each book ordered and add to your total for payment. (*Note: VA residents, I will pay your state tax on each item ordered so you pay less.)

Send checks or cash for this amount to...

Fred First
1020 Goose Creek Run N.E.
Check, VA 24072
contact fred at fred1st@gmail.com

TOTAL AMOUNT
including shipping:

$_____

Thanks!

Please complete the reverse side of this form and add your
mailing address below:

Mail this order from Goose Creek Press to:

Name: _____

Street Address _____

City/State: _____

Please also include an email address if possible so I can contact
you about your order if necessary.

Email: _____

Print more order forms from the web site, slowroadhome.com

*Indicate on this form if you want your book or books inscribed to
someone in particular.*

Goodbyes are not so hard when you remember it is the time we spent together that will last.

www.ingramcontent.com/pod-product-compliance
Lightning Source LLC
Chambersburg PA
CBHW022016090426
42739CB00006BA/152